DEDICATION

This is dedicated to the lovely people I have known at various naturist clubs and resorts all over the world, particularly the good people at Fiveacres Club in Hertfordshire, England.

CW01501067

Kelly Dixon

ACKNOWLEDGEMENTS

To all those who have helped and assisted with this
book. Thank you.
Special thanks to Nudist UK
https://NudistUK.com

How to Become
a Naturist

Kelly Dixon

CONTENTS

WHO IS THIS BOOK FOR?

Single males – Discover the secret to being accepted at naturist clubs and find out where to meet naturist friends – and possibly find romance! Learn how to integrate yourself into the naturist social scene, and also find out where the best nudist beaches and clubs are.

Single females – Find out the best – and safest – way to enter the world of naturism, and where to go if you want to avoid unwelcome attention. Be guided towards the best places to go naked for the first time, in the UK and elsewhere.

Couples – Discover the best clubs and locations for mind-blowing naked holidays, and find out where to meet find other like-minded couples. This book also contains advice for couples who are tempted to join the swinging scene, and tells you the location of beaches where anything can go…

Everyone – Discover how to lose your fears about losing your clothes! This book will help you on your first naturist outing, tell you where the best places are for the first-timer, teach you about essential etiquette when joining a naturist club, and highlight the health benefits of being a naturist!

INTRODUCTION

When I started to write this book, I realised how difficult it was to find the right tone for the subject, because naturism means different things to different people. I didn't want to use too many clichés about naturism, such as the naked man barbecuing sausages, or nude women playing volleyball (both of which do actually happen), but at the same time I didn't want the book to be stuffy or pompous. I have met too many naturists who take the subject of naturism (and themselves) way too seriously.

I hope you find this book interesting, informative and funny (in parts), and I sincerely hope it will help to answer any questions you have about naturism – it may even challenge your existing beliefs...

Most of all, I hope you enjoy the book. I think you will, because the simple fact that you are reading it shows you already have some sort of interest or curiosity in the subject, and perhaps you want to explore it further – or maybe you are already an experienced naturist who wants to learn more.

This book deals with all aspects of the nude experience, from being a 'closet naturist' to experiencing a world which is much less innocent, as well as everything in between.

After you have read this, I don't expect you to immediately tear off your clothes and run around your house naked, but I hope that you will at least consider the idea that naturism would benefit and nourish you – and could also give you a wonderful escape, for a while, from this busy, noisy world.

Nude humour

Two old ladies were sitting on Brighton beach when a completely naked man walked by.

One of the old ladies suddenly had a stroke... but the other couldn't reach!

CHAPTER 1: WELCOME TO NATURISM!

We inhabit a strange planet on which very little has made sense in recent times, from unusual presidential elections to horrendous terrorist activity worldwide. People's lives are changing.

In addition, many people have also been directly affected by recession, stress at work, and the fear of an apparent breakdown in law and order in parts of the world, as well as all the normal everyday pressures and stresses.

The human race has probably never had to deal with so much. This is reflected in a 'me, me, rush rush' kind of society where people are almost sacrificing their souls in order to achieve a better life – whatever they think the 'better life' is.

Many people are also searching for ways to find inner peace, so that they feel as though they are actually living, not just existing. They are also asking, 'How can I escape from life's demands so that my mind, body and soul can feel calm and content?'

Enthusiasts out there will immediately suggest that perhaps yoga is the way to go.

With its combination of healthy exercise and mind-stabilising meditation, it does seem that yoga has many answers – but naturism has plenty as well.

Naturism is like an alternative medicine. It offers an escape from a busy, stressful life. It somehow allows you to switch off your body and brain. It also helps your whole being to feel rejuvenated and invigorated.

nearly dry by the time you reach your beach towel? That's a huge plus by itself!

Just imagine walking on grass completely naked. It's an amazing experience.

These are just a very few of the reasons that people become naturists – and of course there is also the added attraction of the all-over tan, which for many people is another primary reason for entering the world of naturism.

There is something beautifully narcissistic about looking in the mirror after sunbathing naked and enjoying a view of yourself with no 'tramlines' or white bits – no white willy, no white boobs, no white bum…

Doesn't it feel and look better if you are brown all over? Sexier, even..

At this point, some readers will be shouting, 'What about skin damage?'

Some naturists believe that the best protection from the sun is just to have a sun tan in the first place; others have a more cautious and sensible approach. Be on the safe side – always. it is imperative that you keep your skin safe by liberally applying suntan lotion with a high sun protection factor, particularly if you are a 'new nudist' and there may be parts of your body that have never ever seen the sun!

After your skin is used to the sun, you can then start to use lower factors – but I am no expert, so please, please conduct your own research and keep yourself healthy and safe.

There is an abundance of advice and information on the internet about caring for your skin in the sun – which sunscreen to use, how to avoid aging, and much more.

I know of plenty of naturists who are happy to stay out of the sun, emerging from the shade occasionally to have a dip in the pool and then retreating to their sanctuary under a tree or an umbrella.

Also, you should ensure that you have a good moisturiser for use after sunbathing – the last thing you want is dry skin that turns all scabby and flakes off. This applies particularly if you have been on the beach, where the salt water can play havoc with skin.

I should also add that a good diet is helpful for healthy skin, and your health in general, and keep that big bottle of water handy!

You can find further information at Wikihow.com/Look-after-your-skin

- Other helpful websites are available!

The first time I went to a naturist club, I thought I'd been transported to another world. Everyone was completely relaxed – much more than they would have been on a conventional clothed holiday.

Work, stress, and the world's problems felt a million miles away. I embraced the sensation of total liberation and felt at home in this strange, new, exciting but very comfortable culture.

Years later, I feel exactly the same. Nothing has changed.

When I have had an enjoyable afternoon sunning myself by the pool, and then have to drive back out through the gates of my local naturist club to rejoin the real world, it feels as though a wonderful film at the cinema has come to an end, and I have to re-enter a harsh grey reality – or it feels like leaving the beautiful sand of a nudist beach to return to Textile Town, where clothes are mandatory and freedom has been curtailed.

There is something about being in a naturist environment that feels beneficial to the soul. A bit like chicken soup, it feels good, wholesome and kind.

Nude humour

Sign on a nudist beach for pensioners:
'Look out for golden oldies!'

How do you become a naturist?

Surely that's easy. You just take off your clothes!

However, 'just taking off your clothes' is not really the definition or the spirit of naturism; that's just being naked or nude. Otherwise we would all technically be naturists every time we showered or had a bath!

So what is the difference between being a nudist and a naturist?

A nudist is someone who just enjoys being naked, a naturist is also someone who also enjoys being naked but sees nudity more as a lifestyle or culture.

On the internet there are some slightly varying ideas about the meaning of naturism. Here are a couple:

'Naturism or nudism is a cultural and political movement advocating and defending social nudity in private and in public.' - Wikipedia

'Naturism is a way of life in harmony with nature characterised by the practise of communal nudity, with the intention of encouraging self-respect, respect for others and the environment.' – The International Naturist Federation

My own definition of naturism would be similar:

'A naked lifestyle which encompasses nature, peace and freedom, respect for self and the environment.'

The literal meaning of the word 'naturism' doesn't really matter; it's what the lifestyle is about that is important.

Haven't you ever, during the warm summer months, taken off your shoes and enjoyed the feeling of your bare feet against the grass or sand?

Of course you have! It almost feels as if your whole being is connected to nature as your naked skin connects to the surface of the earth.

Think about how you feel generally when swimming – in the sea particularly. Now imagine that the barrier of clothing has been removed. You have no swimsuit on; there is just you, and you can feel the water enveloping your body.

This gives a sense of affinity between yourself and nature which can make you feel as if any problems that you may be experiencing have evaporated. It's just you blending with the sea. Nothing else matters. It's a truly wonderful experience.

Similarly, how relaxing it is to sit back and enjoy the rays of the sun, which seem to penetrate your very being and make you feel happy and calm. But how much better is the sensation when you are completely naked!

Go on, just imagine it – that wonderful feeling of total freedom with the air and sun nourishing your skin, your body unfettered by any form of clothing, allowing nature and you to combine together. The sun can warm every bit of your skin after you've been in the water, and you don't have to put up with a damp, clingy swimsuit and annoying droplets of water trickling everywhere.

How many times have you been swimming and then had to wait for ages for your costume to dry? How much better it is to stroll out of the sea and be nearly dry by the time you reach your beach towel? That's a huge plus by itself!

Just imagine walking on grass completely naked. It's an amazing experience.

These are just a very few of the reasons that people become naturists – and of course there is also the added attraction of the all-over tan, which for many people is another primary reason for entering the world of naturism.

There is something beautifully narcissistic about looking in the mirror after sunbathing naked and enjoying a view of yourself with no 'tramlines' or white bits – no white willy, no white boobs, no white bum…

Doesn't it feel and look better if you are brown all over? Sexier, even..

At this point, some readers will be shouting, 'What about skin damage?'

Some naturists believe that the best protection from the sun is just to have a sun tan in the first place; others have a more cautious and sensible approach. Be on the safe side – always. it is imperative that you keep your skin safe by liberally applying suntan lotion with a high sun protection factor, particularly if you are a 'new nudist' and there may be parts of your body that have never ever seen the sun!

After your skin is used to the sun, you can then start to use lower factors – but I am no expert, so please, please conduct your own research and keep yourself healthy and safe.

There is an abundance of advice and information on the internet about caring for your skin in the sun – which sunscreen to use, how to avoid aging, and much more.

I know of plenty of naturists who are happy to stay out of the sun, emerging from the shade occasionally to have a dip in the pool and then retreating to their sanctuary under a tree or an umbrella.

Also, you should ensure that you have a good moisturiser for use after sunbathing – the last thing you want is dry skin that turns all scabby and flakes off. This applies particularly if you have been on the beach, where the salt water can play havoc with skin.

I should also add that a good diet is helpful for healthy skin, and your health in general, and keep that big bottle of water handy!

You can find further information at Wikihow.com/Look-after-your-skin

- Other helpful websites are available!

naturists, as the name implies they are only seen out naked when the weather is good.

If you wish, you can become just a part-time holiday naturist, and by doing this you will still gain enormous relief from stress.

Simply by shedding your clothes on a nudist beach or in a nudist area, and relaxing properly, could lead to benefits to your well-being and mental health. When you return to work – and real life – after your nudist holiday experience, you should find yourself able to perform at work in a far more effective manner, having experienced true and deep seated relaxation.

However, I can guarantee that you will be counting down the days to your next naturist vacation, and will find yourself on the internet looking at different clothes-free holiday options for the future!

A 'normal' beach-style holiday will never feel the same again! At this stage, you may want to do more and more naturist-based activities such as nudist swims or socialising at your nearest naturist club. Life for you will have changed dramatically.

You might have a brand-new circle of naturist friends who you met on holiday and want to keep in touch, which leads to a problem: what the hell do you say to other people about your nude holiday experience?

What happens when your original non-naturist friends ask you what you did on your holiday? Are you going to be honest?

What happens if you want to invite your new naturist friends to the same occasion or event as your non-naturist friends and family?

Worse still, what happens when your family ask

the same question? Are you going to lie, or try to avoid the truth?

It's tricky. But you're not alone – all naturists have had the same problem.

I am not going to tell you to lie, but often it would be best to keep this new and exciting part of your life to yourself.

You may want to share this part of your life with your bestie, who *of course* you trust not to tell other people... *Of course* they'll understand your new hobby. *Of course* they'll embrace it and want to try it out with you...

No, they probably won't. It's not going to happen.

They are going to look at you in horror. They are going to part your hair and search for the three sixes etched on your skull. They are not going to believe that the person they think they know has become a naturist.

Of course, it's possible that they may greet your news with a 'Really? That's brave of you!' before picking up the phone to other friends after you've gone: *'Have you heard the latest?'*

Whenever I've mentioned my naturist activities to people, the reactions I've had have ranged from total incredulity and disbelief to unsure acceptance.

On one occasion when I was sitting on a nudist beach, I phoned an acquaintance to have a general chat, and halfway through the conversation when I told her where I was, she said: 'What? Are you actually naked talking to me now? - What, actually talking to me with no clothes on?' This was despite the fact that I had already told her that I was a naturist.

So it may be a tough decision for you. Some

friends *may* take it in their stride, but please don't assume that everyone will.

There are also practical reasons why you shouldn't broadcast your new hobby or lifestyle – for example, if you have a job or profession that commands a degree of respect, such as a lawyer or doctor. If people know you are a naturist your credibility may be compromised – not because you are doing anything wrong, but because society doesn't choose to accept it, at the moment.

In February 2017 head teacher Christine Wright appeared in a Channel 4 documentary about naturism called *The Great British Skinny Dip*. Afterwards, someone anonymously allegedly rang Christine's employer and 'outed' her as a nudist. Eventually, she was forced to resign.

What a pity. She came across as a kind, sweet soul, and I'll bet she did a great job at her school.

She now works with Andrew Welch, who at the time had a senior position with British Naturism, and also appeared in the same documentary.

It's an enjoyable and interesting view on organised naturism and naturist activities.

In the documentary Andrew tries to persuade his new partner Sheryn to strip off in public for the first time. The camera shows Sheryn's initial reluctance to get completely nude, but you then almost expect a trumpet fanfare when a proud Andrew and his partner walk naked into a public arena, side by side.

You have to admire people such as Christine, Andrew and Sheryn and others who are – literally – exposing themselves to potential ridicule, scorn and judgement which seems totally unfair – their only agenda is to encourage others to get naked and share the enjoyable experience of being a naturist. Nothing more, nothing less.

They're not being paid to be attacked by the media and the public; they simply believe in this great lifestyle.

They believe that naturism should be practised by more people across the world, for all the reasons listed in this book and more, and, unlike the vast majority of naturists and people in general, they are not afraid to put their heads above the parapet and say:-

'This is me – this is who I am!'

I know naturists from all walks of life and working in all professions.

There are members of the clergy, a dentist, a casino manager, numerous high-powered business people, a couple of teachers, insurance sales people – the list is endless. Sadly, some of these people would be mortified to have their friends, family or work colleagues know they enjoy naturism in their own spare time.

While I was reading an online article about the Great British Skinny Dip documentary, I scanned the viewers' comments that followed the article, and was delighted to observe that, as well as the usual small-brained vitriol, there were an equal number of positive comments, so maybe the tide is turning.

Nude humour

There was a woman who used to play poker at the casino every Saturday night, and she was getting concerned that she always woke her husband up when she got home. So she decided she would be more considerate and try not to wake him in future. So she got undressed in the lounge and then tiptoed into the bedroom, totally naked – only to find her husband sitting up in bed reading.

He looked at her in horror. 'Oh my God!' he exclaimed. 'Did you lose everything?'

CHAPTER 4: HOW IT ALL BEGAN

Naturism as a concept has been around forever, but at the beginning of the twentieth century a Dr Heinrich Pudor carried out a study to find a link between health and exercising while naked. He wrote under the pseudonym Dr Heinrich Scham. Apparently he coined the term *Nacktkultur* ('naked culture').

There followed various other studies in Germany that also advocated the benefits of nudity. In addition, two French physicians studied the effects of natural food and the natural environment on human well-being, and called the concept 'Naturisme'.

Because being out in the fresh air and sunlight also had beneficial effects for people, nudism became part of naturism – and naturism was born.

In the early part of the twentieth century, the first naturist club opened in Hamburg, Germany. It was called *Freilichtpark* ('The Free Light Park'). The concept of naturism then spread to France and the UK and then to the USA, where it became established during the 1930s.

In the early 1950s, the International Naturist Federation was detailed to put pressure on local authorities to allow certain beaches to be used by naturists – and the rest, as they say, is history.

Many famous people throughout history have been known for being nudists, including Agatha Christie and Ernest Hemingway. Apparently Winston Churchill, too, was a nudist and allegedly would sometimes hold court to some of his Cabinet while in the bath.

More recently, journalists have made alleged links

between naturism and some famous actors and celebrities, including Dame Helen Mirren, Brad Pitt, Billy Connolly and Robbie Williams, so we are in good company!

CHAPTER 5: MY FIRST EXPERIENCE

Many, many people have written accounts of their first experiences of naturism. You can read some later on in this book and also at the Nudist UK website NudistUK.com/nudist-stories.

Some people have become naturists by accident; other people have had more of a journey. But the interesting thing is that very few people enter the world of naturism and then leave. Most people who become naturists continue in some form or other for the rest of their lives.

It's always interesting, and sometimes quite sweet, at our local naturist club to observe first-timers. We all feel a degree of empathy for the newbie slowly shuffling out of their clothes and exposing their bare skin to the elements in front of others for the very first time. I sometimes feel as though I want everyone around the pool to give the nervous newbie a hearty round of applause, but maybe that would put them off for life!

I can still clearly remember my very first time. It was at a naturist club in Kent called Eureka. I had managed to catch a lift to the club with a couple of people, who turned out to be seasoned naturists. On arrival, my new friends immediately divested themselves of their clothes and went to the swimming pool leaving me, still clothed, sitting on my towel, looking warily around, feeling as if everyone was staring at me.

I was in my early twenties. Apart from feeling fearful and insecure, I was conscious that everyone around me was naked and looked happy basking in the sun, so I very slowly peeled off my clothes and, still sitting, shuffled out of my jeans. I felt totally exposed – to potential ridicule, judgement and God knows what – feeling the novel sensation of fresh air circulating around my nether regions.

After about five minutes of sitting on the towel clutching my knees, it dawned on me that no one was taking a blind bit of notice of me, despite me being naked. It further dawned on me that I felt, well, *different*. Sort of liberated. Still scared, but not in a bad way. It was a very hot day. People were splashing in the pool, and I felt compelled to join in. Without thinking about it anymore, I ran towards the pool, jumped in and that was it. I effectively become a naturist from that point onwards.

I can honestly say, hand on heart, that that was it. It was like flicking on a switch. After those few short minutes I no longer saw bits, boobs and bottoms, I just saw people. Naked people, yes, but just people. I quickly learned that all sorts of people make up the naturist universe, from every single walk of life: they were all there, nude and content.

Almost immediately I felt as if I had 'crossed over'. I had gone from being the judge to the judged, and I didn't care. I had found my tribe.

I spent the rest of the afternoon relishing this new-found freedom. My two new friends turned out to be a mother and daughter who had been members at the club for many years. In the evening there was a nude disco. I must admit, it did seem a bit weird at first, seeing all these naked people dancing around, penises and breasts flapping everywhere, but there was a great atmosphere and everyone joined in.

I became a regular visitor to the club and had some good times there and met some great people from all walks of life.

After leaving the club and going about my normal daily life again, it felt as though I had joined some sort of gigantic worldwide secret club – which in many ways I had. Whenever I went to a naturist club, it felt like entering an exciting secret world, within which another version of me could emerge.

After my maiden visit I went to the club on a semi-regular basis and got to know other people who frequented the club during the day. They had some things in common: they all seemed very peaceful and at one with themselves. I never saw anything subversive.

One of the strangest things I found was that when I socialised with nudists outside the club – in a clothed, 'normal' situation – there was still a sort of closeness between us. I don't mean in a sexual way, but in an intimate, in-depth way. It was as if we had almost looked into each other's souls. At naturist clubs there is no need for secrets or bullshit; your character is exposed, along with your skin. It feels healthy and good.

Naked conversations reflect that same quality. While you're sunbathing at a naturist club and chatting to others, people don't seem to feel they need to be pretend to be someone they're not. There is little artifice. People feel they can be themselves – neither their psychological nor their physical shortcomings are covered up. Our conversations were as honest as ones you would have with your best friend, sometimes even deeper.

I fell away from naturism for a few years for various reasons, but then returned to it almost gleefully, having missed it dreadfully.

This time around, I was living near London. I became a member of, and regular visitor to, the wonderful Fiveacres Club in Hertfordshire. The Fiveacres Club is in Bricket Wood and is set, despite the name, in 7 acres of grounds. It offers all you could want from a naturist club. There is a sauna, mini-tennis, boules, a lovely outdoor pool and a clubhouse with sun terraces. Fiveacres was one of the first naturist clubs in the UK and has a long and varied history – worthy of a book on its own.

It was easy to make friends at Fiveacres, because the people were so friendly, and the two people who ran the club, Pat and Ian, had the attitude of 'Be peaceful and don't upset others', which suited me perfectly. Just as I had felt at Eureka years before, when entering the gates of the club, it felt like a calm oasis, the best stress relief ever. Sometimes during the summer, when I was working in the city during the day, I would look forward to the evening when I could disappear to Fiveacres and jump into the pool.

Even on cooler evenings, simply stripping off and relaxing naked for an hour or so was enough to charge my batteries.

I also went on various naturist holidays, most of which had been recommended to me by other club members at Fiveacres, and I will pass on some of those recommendations later.

Spielplatz is a naturist club that dates back to 1929 – it is one of the oldest clubs in the UK. It is located in St Albans close to the Fiveacres site, and was featured in a TV documentary called *The Naked Village*. Spielplatz, which means 'playground' in German, is far more of a community than most other naturist sites, in that the place is home to around 50 full-time residents. (The site was originally bought for the princely sum of £500 – nowadays it is considered to be worth around 12 million because of the site's value to potential property and land developers.)

All the naturist clubs I have visited have been welcoming and friendly, and all clubs offer something different.

Some clubs concentrate on the catering side of the business and offer sumptuous food; others offer hotel rooms on-site for visitors who are too weary or worse for wear to get home after a party or event.

Silverleigh Naturist Club in West Kingsdown, Kent, is a good example: it has a fine selection of double rooms, some of which are en-suite, at very reasonable prices.

Some clubs offer camping or camper van facilities. If you'd like more information, contact your local club. You are not being a nuisance (unless of course you *are* a nuisance!).

This book ends by listing all the naturist clubs I could find in the UK. It only takes a phone conversation to see if your local naturist club is the one for you. If it's not, you may have to travel further afield. I know many naturists who quite happily travel around 50 miles to regularly visit their favourite naturist club. Sometimes they stay over and make a weekend of it.

Nude humour

Sign outside a naturist club: 'Sorry, clothed for winter!'

CHAPTER 6: COMMON FEARS OF THE NEW NUDIST

Will my body be judged?

I'm worried about my stretch marks!

Will people think my boobs are too small – or too big?

Does my body size matter to other naturists?

I am too fat/too thin/I have a birthmark/Will I feel embarrassed taking my clothes off?/Is my penis big enough?/Will people stare at me?

Most naturists accept and love diversity in others, so if you are worried about being overweight or believe your body is not perfect (whose is?), stop worrying. You will be in excellent company.

Most naturists don't look like models, but they don't care. Similarly, they don't particularly care what *your* body looks like.

What they do care about is that you are a friendly person who will fit in to the group – or at the very least you won't disrupt the group's peace and harmony in any way. They're more concerned about what kind of person you are on the inside.

As far as birthmarks, stretch marks, artificial limbs and missing limbs are concerned, yes, people are bound to notice, but they are unlikely to stare. Seasoned naturists have seen it all before; they just want to enjoy their own naked experience.

I have seen a few women on nudist beaches and at naturist clubs who have had mastectomy surgery and if anything appear to wear their scars with pride.

The two most commonly asked questions on the Nudist UK website relate to (1) penis size – and (2) what happens if men get an erection in response to other people's nudity.

Let's take penis size first (the elephant in the room for many) and get it out of the way. As far as sex is concerned, some people prefer their partner to have a larger penis, and some prefer a smaller or average-sized penis. It's all a matter of taste. (Unintentional pun – sorry)

This statement is not intended to make the less endowed feel better; it's just a fact.

Also, trust me when I say that whilst I can fully understand what it's like to feel nervous in front of others, and can appreciate the fact that many people's shortcomings are in the mind, as well as the body perhaps, but the vast majority of people at a nudist club will not give a damn what size your penis is, so please don't worry about it. There is too much else to enjoy in the world of naturism, as I hope *you'll* discover.

Naturism as a philosophy has nothing at all to do with sex, and that is reflected in the way that naturists view each other. It's as if bare skin is a form of clothing or attire. After a while, you just don't notice each other's nudity, and you certainly don't judge each other. Think about it. It is clothes that sexualise people, not nudity. When you are about to make love with your partner, it is the intimacy that is the turn-on, not necessarily the nakedness.

On a nudist beach, or even around the pool at the club, the only time you'll notice anyone paying attention to other nudists is when they are taking their clothes off. I have often seen men's interest levels increase as a woman is disrobing. As soon as she is naked, the man loses interest and goes back to his book or whatever.

And it doesn't just apply to men. I've observed women clocking men in the same manner, only to look away when they have seen what they wanted to see.

I've often been asked, 'How do you stop yourself continually watching naked women? Aren't you perpetually turned on?'

The answer is 'No. Once you've noticed someone's naked body for the first time, you just tune out afterwards and nakedness becomes the new norm. And that's only if you really notice it in the first place.'

I know it's hard to believe, but it's true. Once you've seen a body, then you've seen it! There is no real desire to keep looking at it. Naturists will understand this straight away, but textiles (non-naturists) will struggle with this information until they try naturism for themselves. Then they will see what I mean!

I've had many conversations over the years about this very subject. One day, I was sitting with several others on the patio at the Fiveacres Club. We had spent a chilled-out Sunday lounging by the pool, and a few of us had decided to wander to the clubhouse bar for a few early evening drinks before heading off. It had got a little chilly after the heat of the day, so two of the women there had put their clothes on while chatting. One of the women was wearing a short summer dress and was sitting opposite the men.

One of the men suddenly exclaimed, 'Bloody hell, I don't believe I just did that!'

'What are you talking about?' the woman in the dress asked.

'Well,' he said, 'I've been talking to you all afternoon, and I've known you for years, so I've seen every single bit of you, but right now you're fully clothed, you just crossed your legs, and I tried to sneak a peek up your dress. How ridiculous is that!'

'I know what you mean,' said another man. 'I live here and obviously see nudity all the time, but the other day I was driving in town and I passed a girl on a bike who was wearing a very short skirt, and I drove around the block a couple of times just to get a look.'

Then one of the women said, 'Well, I look too. It's hard not to. You always want to see something that you're not supposed to see.'

And there it is in a nutshell. *You want to see the things that you're not supposed to see*, so when you are in an intimate situation for the first time with someone new, there is always a sense of daring, a sense of heady excitement, that you're seeing something that has previously been hidden from you.

Once your partner has removed their clothing and you are encountering bare flesh, that excitement is replaced by a sense of intimacy.

Hopefully this has in some way illustrated why naturists don't walk around in a state of perpetual sexual excitement, it just doesn't work that way.

What you look like naked, or what your penis size is, makes little difference to naturists, they care about being relaxed and happy at their club or beach, and will probably care that the sun is shining.

In a similar vein, let's get to the other big question that I've been asked so many times which is: 'Will I get an erection when I see other people naked?'

No, you almost definitely won't, partly for the reasons already mentioned and for the fact that on your first visit to a naturist club or beach, you are likely to be experiencing an emotion somewhere between 'terrified' and a 'bit nervous' than 'aroused', which is hardly conducive for an erection. Later on, as you become more relaxed in your surroundings, if it does happen just do the gentlemanly thing and cover it up or lie on your belly, or go for a swim and cool off.

People won't judge you for getting an erection – they may even think it's funny if it is a one-off and you're trying to disguise the fact it's happened – but they will definitely judge you, and not in a good way, if you start waving it around or deliberately draw attention to it. It's a sure-fire way of getting yourself thrown out of the club forever, or becoming persona non grata on the beach.

While naturists don't generally take any notice of each other's bits and pieces, they do sometimes admire others' bodies – as they would if they were wearing clothes. A nicely toned male body, for example, will draw admiring glances, as will a shapely female form. And, yes, an attractive pair of breasts or a particularly well-shaped penis or bum may create some interest, but people do not generally judge.

In my experience, most people actually become more confident as a direct result of naturism. They are generally less body conscious and less judgemental about themselves and others. It is wonderfully liberating not to care whether someone is wearing clothes or not.

I have often sat with another couple at our local naturist club, having a chat and a drink, and afterwards I have genuinely been unable to remember whether they were clothed or unclothed on that occasion – you get to the stage where it really doesn't matter!

A woman was finishing having a shower when the doorbell rang. The woman wrapped a towel around her and answered the door. A friend of her husband stood there. He looked at her and said, 'Oh, sorry, I obviously got you out of the shower. Is your husband in?'

She said, 'No, he'll be back soon.'

'Okay,' he said. 'Do you mind me telling you that you have wonderful skin?'

'No, not at all,' she said, pleased.

'If I gave you £100, would you remove the towel from your upper body – just for five seconds?' he asked.

She thought, 'This is easy money, why not?' So she exposed the top half of her body for five seconds.

'That's fantastic!' exclaimed the man. 'Now would you consider taking the towel off altogether for another £100?'

'This is money for old rope!' she thought, and dropped the towel to the floor.

The man had a good look, complimented her on her body, and gave her £200.

Later on, her husband came home. She mentioned that his mate had come round earlier.

'Brilliant,' he said. 'Did he give you the £200 he owes me?'

CHAPTER 7: THE NUDIST BEACH

As a nervous newbie or budding naturist, you might think it would be easier to take your clothes off for the first time on a nudist beach rather than at a naturist club. Your reasons are likely to be:

- I'm less likely to bump into someone I know, especially if the beach is in another country.
- I'll probably never see the people around me ever again.
- There is no membership fee to pay.
- I don't feel that I have to make social contact with anyone.

All of these are true, of course but there are potential disadvantages to making your first time at a nudist beach. For example:

- Someone may be using a camera or phone camera to capture images.
- You are more likely to be hassled by a stranger.
- There is likely to be people on the beach, who are non-nudists (or 'textiles'), which – strangely – is a bit uncomfortable.
- Will there be facilities – toilets, a bar, a café?
- How safe is it for swimming?
- There are no locked gates, fences or barriers, which is great for access, but it means that *anyone* can wander onto a nudist beach, including people who have no interest in

joining in with social nudity but who just want to either stare at, or hassle, others on the beach.

One time I was sunbathing naked on Brighton nudist beach which is situated just before the marina.

It was a seriously hot day, and a friend and I were lying on the pebbles enjoying the heat and looking forward to having a dip in the sea. All of a sudden, a shadow was cast over us, blocking out the sun. We opened our eyes to see a huge man looming over us, fully clothed and wearing a thick black overcoat! Apart from the fact that he was wearing winter attire on such a hot day, he was only a couple of metres from us and was staring intently in our direction, his gaze unwavering. It was completely unnerving. He said nothing; he just stood there watching us.

It was my friend's first time naked on a beach, so she covered herself and hunched forward nervously. Because I was more seasoned, I told the man to bugger off in no uncertain terms, a sentiment thankfully echoed by all the sun worshippers around us, and he went back up along the beach, hopefully not bothering anyone else.

Now, I realise it is possible that he had a mental health issue, but it was my friend's first foray into naturism, and he could easily have put her off forever. As it turned out, it didn't, and to this day she is a huge fan. Apart from this incident on Brighton beach, I have never had a problem on any naturist beach anywhere in the world. It should be noted that Brighton beach is extremely accessible – by anyone. You only have to walk (or catch the mini-train) up to the far end of the beach, nearly as far as the Marina, step onto the pebbles and you are there!

This makes it very easy for people who just want to gawp at naked bodies. Most naturist beaches are the complete opposite – they can be very inaccessible. In many cases, some people would argue that they are *too* inaccessible, especially for those who are disabled or wheelchair bound.

This makes the naturist club a good choice for first-time nudists. Not only is there likely to be more facilities for disabled people, but the chance of being bothered by someone is virtually nil.

Most naturist clubs' staff and management will have empathy for first-timers, and will help and guide the newbie through the process.

So which is best for the first-timer – the nudist beach or the naturist club? The nudist beach has huge benefits – the sand and the sea and the lovely views can't be replicated in a naturist club. Also, naturist beaches are not that communal. You turn up, pick your spot, and sometimes spend the day sunbathing without talking to anyone else – which is great if that's what you want. It means that you can truly relax and enjoy the day with no interruption.

On the other hand, naturist clubs have all the benefits I mentioned above, and you can enjoy total privacy from the outside world and use the club's facilities.

You are also more likely to strike up a conversation at a club rather than the beach. Having said that, I have made many holiday friends starting from casual conversations held on naturist beaches throughout the world, including France, Spain and the Canary Islands, and some not so well known places such as Little Palm beach on Waiheke Island which is off the coast of New Zealand, near Auckland.

But you don't have to travel too far to enjoy great nudist beaches. I have already mentioned Brighton beach (which, for me, is too pebbly and public, but is a great convenient naturist beach if you live within striking distance).

Travel further along the south coast and you will come to Fairlight Glen beach in Hastings (also known as Covehurst Bay). It is difficult to access, but is absolutely ideal for the first-timer. If you have never stripped off on a beach before, then this is the place for you. This beach is scattered with large boulders that afford a privacy for the nervous or first-time naturist. The beach is difficult to find, and impossible to reach directly by road – you get to it by walking down through a wood, which is actually really pleasant. It is mainly dedicated nudists who frequent the beach.

Warning: it feels like a long trek back to the car afterwards. It's definitely not for the faint-hearted!

A more popular naturist beach on the south coast of England is Studland beach near Bournemouth. It is a lovely long sandy beach that is backed by dunes. The beach is in two parts – textile and naturist – the two separated by a warning sign. The beach is accessible by road, and there is parking (although when you have parked you have to walk through the textile part of the beach before you reach the naturist area).

There are probably shortcuts to get to the naturist area more quickly, and I'm sure that you could ask one of the regular sun worshippers there. Swimming at Studland is an absolute joy because the sea floor slopes very gently and you have to stride out a long way to get in any deeper, making it ideal for games and family fun, and gentler swims.

Studland has had its share of adverse publicity in recent years, mainly about sexual activity and voyeurism in the dunes behind the beach, but the true nudist contingent, along with the local authorities, are doing their best to stamp out any inappropriate behaviour.

If you like big, deserted beaches and fancy something wilder, there are some beaches in Wales that can give other beaches anywhere in the world a run for their money. Check out Kenfig Burrows (also known as Sker beach) near Porthcawl in Bridgend: it's a huge beach with a tiny, and unofficial, naturist area. But what a lovely long walk it is through Kenfig National Nature Reserve to get to the stunning beach, followed by about a half-mile wander along the sands to the right, where the naturist area is. There are no warning signs, and you could easily miss the area because a lot of the regular naturists (who are mostly men) burrow into the dunes above that part of the beach.

Local dog walkers seem quite used to nudists making a mad dash into the waves, and tend not take much notice.

To be respectful, when sunbathing, many naturists perform a temporary cover-up when any clothed people draw near, and politely wave hello as they go past.

This has been a quick introduction to a very few of the nudist beaches in the UK. There are many other naturist beaches, official and unofficial, hidden and otherwise, and searching the internet will give you more idea of beaches close to you, reviews of them, their locations and facilities.

There are very also many fine naturist beaches throughout Europe, particularly in Spain, the Canary Islands and parts of France. You can enjoy long naked walks along miles of sandy beach without seeing anyone else.

In addition, there are many deserted coves and beaches that are ideal for those trying nudism for the first time.

Be aware that sometimes the combination of nudity and the holiday atmosphere is too much for those with healthy libidos, and we have often been walking along a beach, or through dune areas, and have come across an amorous couple in the throes of passion.

As you become a more experienced naturist you might, fortunately or unfortunately, depending on your view, discover beaches and places where wholesale sexual activity is carried out quite openly. Again, more about this, and naturist holidays generally, later.

Nude humour

A young lady was arrested for wearing a two-piece outfit while walking on Eastbourne Pier. She was just wearing socks!

CHAPTER 8: JOINING A NATURIST CLUB

Joining a naturist club is one of the best ways of starting your journey into naturism. As already mentioned, the management will be sympathetic to you as a newbie, and will do everything they can to make you feel welcome and part of the club.

Sometimes a locker and changing area will be available where, just like a superhero, you can walk in clothed, and then burst out in all your naked glory!

The management of a club may introduce new members to a couple of their trusted regulars. This will ensure that the new members are aware of the club's facilities, rules, and social activities and the culture of the club itself.

It also means that the trusted regulars can feed back to the management any useful information about the new members, are they going to fit in? Are they a threat in any way to the club's ethos?

Not everyone is welcome at a naturist club, however. Couples generally are, although sometimes there is a form of vetting process to ensure that they are unlikely to behave in such a way as to bring the club's name into disrepute.

The same applies to single females, but single men are treated by most naturist clubs with an initial wariness and caution. The reasons for this, I'm afraid, are pretty obvious.

It is well known that some men can be a bloody nuisance in situations involving nudity. I'm sure some women can also, but some men can be pests, and it's the club's job to weed out those who just want to perv over naked bodies and use the club and its members for their own gratification.

I'm not sure why, but the words 'naturist club' and 'nudist' appear to make many people think of sexuality and debauchery. They think that, because people are sunbathing naked, there are orgies, bondage sessions and so on taking place. Yes, such clubs exist, but these clubs aren't really the point of being a *naturist club*.

So don't, if you are a single man, phone up your local naturist club and ask if they do sex sessions. Even if they did, do you think they would tell you over the phone?

If you are a single man and want to join a local naturist club, the first thing to remember is to be respectful. When you are applying to any club, you don't have the right to be accepted; you are essentially applying to join a private club. The people in that club will have a common bond, and may be naturally mistrustful of any new additions.

It takes time for any new member – especially a single man – to be fully accepted by the others. Every naturist club has many more membership applications from men than from women, so in the interest of keeping a balance between the sexes, clubs tend to accept fewer men as club members. (The exception to this is clubs that have a sexual undertone, especially on 'special' nights when women are given free entrance and the men have to pay a premium for admission. Which clubs are these? Just get on the internet, find out for yourself, and then please leave genuine naturist clubs well alone. Thanks.)

If you are a single man who wants to join your local club for all the right reasons then the best way to apply is to phone the management and arrange an appointment to view the club. This is quite common, and means that you can take a look at the club's facilities and see if it meets your needs. It also means the club management can take a look at you and see if they like you. It's as simple as that.

It's one thing to be accepted by the club, but it's another to be accepted by the other club members. They will be even more wary of you than the club management. Are you going to be a nuisance? Are you going to encroach on their territory? Make a pass at their wives or partners?

In short, they don't know you, so give them a chance. The best way to settle in is to whilst passing on your way to your chosen sun bathing spot, wave a cheery hello to everyone and then keep yourself to yourself while they adjust to having a new person in their midst.

Don't force yourself on them. Eventually they may want to know a bit about you – such as your name, where you come from, and what job you do. This is natural nosiness intended to find out if you are a risk, or a good person to have as a fellow member.

When you next turn up, they may greet you by name and then you will begin to feel included.

However, don't try to become one of the group too quickly. Most naturists want huge chunks of peace and quiet with the occasional bit of humour thrown around, or a bit of relevant conversation. They don't want someone taking over and interrupting their peace.

Once you are trusted and liked, then a naturist club is the most wonderful place you can visit.

You can become part of the club, and enjoy all the naturist activities available. You will be included in the friendly banter, but this generally doesn't happen straight away.

Take your time, respect everyone, and you will gradually become part of the club community.

Most members of any naturist club can point out to you a visitor or even another member who is perceived as being not particularly welcome at the club. These are usually men who will edge from one person to another, ask how each member is as a conversation opener, and then will talk in a monologue for ten minutes about themselves.

When you are faced with such a person, you feel trapped. You stand, or sit, politely, a fixed smile on your face, waiting for him to finish speaking so that you can continue relaxing in the sun, or whatever.

Don't be that person!

Now that doesn't sound very friendly, I know, but bear in mind that the primary reason for being at a naturist club is to get away from 'normal' daily life and to enjoy your own peace and freedom. So anyone who interrupts that enjoyment is a bloody nuisance.

I realise that many people reading this will say, 'This is all just common sense', but I also know that many of my naturist friends reading this will be saying, 'I know just the person you are talking about!'

By comparison, it seems a simpler process for a single woman to join.

Again, just phone your local club, explain that you would like to come along and view the club and facilities, and ask if there is anyone who could show you around and answer any questions. The club will be more than happy to comply. If you decide to join, you will find that most people at the club will be willing to take you under their wing.

I cannot guarantee that you won't get chatted up at

some stage – this can happen in any situation – but if this happens at a club and someone is becoming a nuisance, all you have to do is alert a member of the club staff or management, and the problem will be sorted out. As I have already mentioned, no one likes pests.

Once they had become members, all the single women I know were perfectly content to come back and forward to the club on their own, and even join in regular social events. I also know a few single women who have pitched or rented caravans on a naturist site and live pretty much as full-time nudists.

Do male and female single nudists ever get together romantically? Yes, all the time. There have been plenty of weddings as a result of couples meeting at a naturist location or event – and sometimes those weddings are truly naturist in that all attending, including the vicar or celebrant, are nude.

I believe there is something truly lovely about baring everything to each other, and friends and family, when making your vows. Most weddings, however, are 'normal' – by which I mean 'clothed'. This is because it is rare for a couple, their family and their friends all to be naturists. Sometimes a couple has a naturist blessing after the official event.

There is more about finding love as a naturist a bit later in this book.

Nude humour

Never try to bathe a cat when you are naked!

CHAPTER 9: NUDIST COUPLES

A new couple joining a naturist club delights everyone. Membership is virtually guaranteed for couples because couples have more credibility, as far as clubs are concerned. Couples are usually warmly welcomed by other members straight away, and many friendships are formed from the very first social event. People will ask the usual social questions: 'How and when did you get into naturism? Do you have a family? Where do you live?'

Couples like to talk and socialise with other couples, and there cannot be, and shouldn't be, (in theory) any jealousy on anyone's part. Sometimes mild flirting between couples is viewed as just a bit of fun, and is even encouraged.

Couples will sit together around the pool and share picnics, drinks and conversation, or meet up at the club's evening social events. Many naturist couples go on holiday with other naturist couples – without being thought of as 'swingers' – and have a fantastic time. I know two couples who, at weekends, share a caravan at their local club and spend their time totally naked. There isn't even the sniff of a rumour that they are swinging; they just enjoy sunbathing and socialising together. They go on holiday together and enjoy each other's company. If the men can't make it then the two women come down on their own; if one of the men can't make it, then the other three come. It is a really healthy situation that works well for them, with absolutely no jealousy on anyone's part.

However, swinging does happen – it's a fact of life. I have never experienced it, or noticed it to any great degree, at any of the clubs I have visited, but it happens!

I know of a couple who used to regularly attend social events at the club and would say quite proudly, 'We're swingers' to anyone and everyone, but only if the conversation wandered in that direction. They were a lovely couple and didn't try to force themselves on anyone; it was just their way of life, and they were very up-front and honest about it.

A few naturist clubs have a reputation for being swinger-oriented, and these are probably not ideal for the inexperienced naturist.

You will get a good idea which these clubs are by simply visiting their website. If you see mentions of 'adult playrooms' or similar, then the club actively targets swingers. Most clubs, however, have quite a strict policy as far as sex is concerned. For example, occasionally a naked couple will get over-amorous in the swimming pool and perhaps be kissing and cuddling in the water. This kind of activity is normally frowned upon by the club, and the offenders will probably be asked to stop and get a room!

The majority of naturist clubs tend to take a dim view of any activity that might affect their member's enjoyment of the premises, and of course any activity that threaten their licence or adversely affect their reputation as a family-safe business.

It's important that all members can bring young families along to also enjoy the facilities without being exposed to anything inappropriate.

Club members are normally aware of the club rules, and will sometimes bring anyone who flout the rules to book, or will refer the culprits to club management.

They are just trying to keep *their* club the way it is. While we all recognise that a couple naked together in a swimming pool may get a little carried away, there is a time and place, and if this was allowed to carry on then it may stop the genuine naturists from attending.

On the other hand, there are a few clubs that have made a transition from being a naturist centre to being a sex orientated club catering for swingers and the like, and these clubs would have a vetting process in place that would dissuade genuine naturists and completely disallow anyone under age.

We will look at naturists and swinging in Chapter 12, along with naturist holidays and locations where swinging takes place, so that you can make your own mind up whether to avoid those places or not. Many naturists complain that swinging at some naturist clubs gives naturism a bad name to the outside world – or at least an inaccurate perception – and they have a point.

As a budding naturist, nervously pondering where to go for your very first time, wouldn't the thought of that kind of activity put you off going to that club? Obviously it depends on the individual.

There are already a whole bunch of people out there who believe that anyone who takes their clothes off in front of strangers must be a pervert.

In fact, one of the most popular questions on the Nudist UK site is '*Do perverts go to naturist clubs?*'

It's a difficult question to answer, because how would anyone know? What does a pervert look like? What does a pervert do that makes him perverted to other people? Does a pervert know themselves that they are a pervert?

Also, what is 'perverted' to some people may be perfectly normal to others. For example, swingers are seen as perverts by some people, and a fun way of life by others, hence the term 'Lifestyle' which is used, mostly in the USA, as the term for 'Swingers.'

One thing is for sure; club history has shown that a pervert, or someone who seems to have a dodgy ulterior motive for being at a naturist club, will, very quickly be outed and barred. It's as simple as that!

Nude humour

A man went into a shop and bought himself a really expensive pair of crocodile-skin shoes. When he got home, he put on the shoes and proudly showed them off to his wife.

'What do you think, love?' he asked.

She said, 'I'm busy – go and watch telly or something'

He thought, 'I'll show her,' so he went upstairs and took all his clothes off except his new shoes, and then went back down and stood in front in front of his wife.

'Now what do you think?' he asked her.

'You're showing off your willy!' she exclaimed.

'Yes,' he exclaimed, 'it's pointing towards my new shoes!'

She replied:-

'Well, you should have got yourself a new hat then!'

CHAPTER 10: THE GOLDEN RULES OF NATURISM

I believe it was the late Mark Wilson, the owner of the Eureka naturist club in Kent, who proudly stated that he had only one rule, his eleventh commandment:

'Thou shalt not annoy!'

You won't go far wrong if you adopt this maxim in any naturist environment.

But there *are* rules at naturist clubs, not just for single people but for everyone, and the first rule is ALWAYS USE A TOWEL WHEN SITTING NAKED on any kind of furniture indoors or outside.

Why? Because nobody likes the idea of putting their bare bottom on a seat where someone else's bare bottom has been! Apart from the fact it is unhygienic, it is also socially unacceptable in naturist circles.

Your towel is your friend. To dry with, lie on, cover up with, or sit on.

Even on a naturist holiday, when eating, people will put a towel down on their chair or put on a wrap-around before sitting down. This is naturist etiquette and must be observed at all times. If you don't do this, you may not be thrown out of the club, but you will incur angry looks and bad feeling from the other members.

There are other rules, which vary from club to club and relate to health and safety: for example, there may be rules around the swimming pool (no diving or pushing others into the water, no swimming after a certain time, etc.). Other rules may relate to smoking, alcohol, footwear, personal jewellery (piercings), the use of mobile phones, photography, inappropriate behaviour, etc. Each club has its own set of rules.

One controversial rule bans swimming costumes in the pool (except for young children, in many clubs), but there are good reasons for this.

First of all, it's a naturist club! The clue is in the name. Why would you want to swim in a costume at a naturist club?

You also run the risk of the local lads football team wanting to join the club and jump around the pool in their shorts, this would definitely hack off the other naturist club members!

Nearly all naturist clubs welcome their members' children of all ages. Why wouldn't they? They could be future naturists and club members! It is wonderful to note that, in my experience, people around the pool will keep half an eye out for the younger children and will quickly alert their parents if they get into difficulties.

Many clubs have a rule that bans 'personal' jewellery – which can mean bodily piercings in the genital area, and sometimes elsewhere. Items like the steel bar that is inserted through the end of a man's penis (known as a Prince Albert) may not be allowed, or metal rings or studs dangling from a woman's labia.

I'm not sure why this rule exists. I have no piercings because it's not my preference and I don't like pain, but other people wear body piercings and jewellery in the same way that people in the outside world would wear accessories such as a watch, earrings or bracelet.

But rules are rules, and perhaps some clubs see

personal body jewellery as a perversion of nudism.

So if you are applying for a new membership at a naturist club, check out the rules first. You may find that tattoos are also unwelcome, although that seems old-fashioned, considering how trendy (and widespread) they now are. I would have thought – and hoped – that naturist clubs would be striving to get new members, not putting up barriers.

Nude humour

A woman is standing totally naked in her bathroom, looking in the mirror. She is not happy with what she sees, and says to her husband in a sad voice, 'I look terrible. I look as though I'm fat, wrinkly, old and ugly… I really need you to pay me a compliment.'

'No problem!' says her husband. 'Your eyesight is brilliant!'

CHAPTER 11: HEALTH BENEFITS OF BEING A NATURIST

Sometimes, when people get older, they fall into an unhealthy lifestyle. Some people spend too much time sitting, inactive, watching too much TV not socialising. Many people are lonely. This can lead to health problems, including anxiety and depression, and poorer self-image, which in turn can lead to 'getting old before your time' and can contribute to a breakdown of mental and physical health.

Once you have begun a sedentary lifestyle, it becomes a habit – and, as we all know, habits are very hard to break. Many over-50s deliberately take up activity-based hobbies such as sailing, badminton, swimming or walking for this very reason. All these activities are excellent forms of exercise, and can be enjoyed as a group which, of course, is in itself highly beneficial.

Younger people can fall into a similar trap – many want to stay indoors whatever the weather, and play computer games, spend hours on social media sites, or watch rubbish television.

Naturism gives people a reason to get out of the house and get the fresh air and exercise they need. When the sun shines, the first thought in many naturists' heads is: 'I want to get to my nearest club and get in the pool,' or 'Let's go down to the beach!'

Swimming is one of the best forms of exercise you can have. Instead of queuing up at the local swimming baths and having to put up with screaming children and a heavy, wet swimsuit, you can put your naturist club membership to good use and enjoy the freedom and comparative tranquillity of the club swimming pool.

I cannot stress enough how enjoyable and relaxing it is to swim naked, whether it's in the pool or the sea, and then to dry off in the sunshine. This has got to be good for the body and soul. Then later, when you look in the mirror, how much better do you look? If you look and feel relaxed, then you feel good.

Many naturist clubs have facilities conducive to good health, such as a sauna, gym, outdoor sports like badminton or bowls, and perhaps a table tennis table.

Food menus in clubs now include healthy options such as salads, jacket potatoes and vegetarian options, normally at a reasonable price.

If the nudist beach is your preference, bearing in mind how far some of them are off the beaten track, the very act of getting to the beach is healthy exercise in itself!

It's important to get out into the open air and enjoy all that nature has to offer. This – enjoying the sun, and even the rain and wind – is, for many people, the most important part of naturism.

However, the social aspect of naturism is also healthy. Keeping those grey cells firing with new shared experiences and conversations with like-minded friends is definitely good for you.

A further benefit of naturism is that you save money (and I don't mean saving money on clothes!) because many naturist activities are free, apart from travel expenses or club memberships.

Some naturists view naturism as a saviour of old age, and I'm sure you can understand why.

Nude humour

A man was sunbathing in the nude and ended up burning his penis. His doctor told him to ease the pain by dipping it into milk. Later, his young wife came home to discover her husband standing with his willy in a saucer of milk.

'Bloody hell!' she exclaimed. 'I always wondered how you reloaded that!'

CHAPTER 12: SWINGING NATURISTS

When you become a member of your local naturist club, you will be invited to join in with social events. These events can be held over Christmas, Easter and on bank holidays, but most events are held on weekends during the summer. Many clubs close their doors during the winter, but some will host occasional events. You will receive a leaflet, email, or there will be a sign at the club advertising what's on.

Events include discos, live bands, quizzes, karaoke nights and themed nights, such as *Pirates of the Caribbean,* Hallowe'en (of course) or 'Tramps and Tarts' – in fact, any excuse to dress up and have some fun. Sometimes, after some alcoholic drinks the fun may descend into chaos, with revellers stripping off and maybe leaping around in the snow, or just enjoying naked horseplay. It's usually harmless fun and the events are normally well attended.

Of course, some clubs encourage, or turn a blind eye to, a bit of sexual activity, and if you have chosen to visit one of these clubs with your partner, other couples will try to sound you out. They will try to find out whether you and your partner/spouse are up for a bit of swapping or hanky-panky.

Now, these people don't have two heads and breathe fire; they are usually very nice people with families who just like to swap partners occasionally. It's no big deal to them; that's their thing.

However, it could – and perhaps should – be a big deal to you.

After a few glasses of wine, it's all too easy to respond to a bit of flattery. Remember going on nights out when you were single? You had a few

relationship for the sake of a quick fling, as tempting it may be at the time.

It's interesting to note that most swingers will also give you the same advice. They don't want to wreck other relationships either.

Nude humour

This elephant looked down to the naked man
confused and asked:
'How do you breathe through that thing?'

CHAPTER 13: STARTING A NATURIST ENTERPRISE

If you Google a number of phrases connected to the word 'naturism' you will discover that while it is obvious that there is a massive interest in the subject, there are comparatively few naturist enterprises.

When a person first becomes a naturist, they may want to learn more about the subject, so they will order/download books on naturism, subscribe to Health & Efficiency, and all of a sudden a new life takes shape, with a naturist theme running through it. Normal everyday activities might now have to encompass nudity – for example, an evening at the pub could be replaced by a night out at the local naturist club; holidays may now be clothes-free; and they make new naturist friends.

In short, naturism becomes a new hobby. While there are many naturist clubs which have fewer members than they used to, naturism itself is on the increase, with naturist parks springing up in Germany and France, as well as enterprises like nude restaurants and nude cycle rides.

All this is great news for someone who wants to start a new business in an alternative niche. According to the British Naturism website there are around four million naturists in the UK, so there are plenty of potential customers.

You could set yourself up as a naturist handy-person, a naturist gardener, freelance naturist photographer, naturist blogger – anything you like, as long as it is legal!

One woman I know started a naked cleaning enterprise in the UK. Her company offers ordinary (clothed) cleans or naked cleans. The ordinary cleaner is charged at a standard rate and naked cleaners are more expensive.

Naked cleaners perform their jobs in exactly the same way as a conventional cleaner, to the satisfaction of their client. They then put on their clothes and leave.

There is definitely no hanky-panky at any stage of the process. Clients are mainly naturists who appreciate there is a 'hands off' policy, that no touching allowed, and they are happy to enjoy a nude cleaner vacuuming carpets and dusting furniture.

She says that her customers are not perverts, but enjoy sitting in their homes naked and don't want to get dressed just because the cleaner has arrived.

There is an interview with her on the Nudist UK website.

If you have a recognised skill or trade, you could become a naturist butler, cook, masseur or masseuse. You could also offer your services as a nude electrician, carpenter or plumber, providing that you don't break any laws relating to health and safety or decency.

There are many naturist clubs and other establishments which are reluctant to engage the services of a normally clothed tradesman, in case any of their patrons are made to feel embarrassed. However, all naturists will happily accept a naked tradesman working in their establishment. It would be seen as normal.

There are actually very few tradespeople who advertise themselves as 'nude-friendly' and target naturist establishments, so you could be amongst the first! Contact your local naturist club or holiday establishment and offer *your* services. They might be grateful to hear from you.

If you are in a band or enjoy playing music to other people, you could be on to a winner. It is very difficult for naturist clubs to find musicians who will perform in the nude. They frequently have to have a clothed band or entertainer, who looks in a bemused fashion at the naked revellers dancing before them.

If you can find the guts to sing or play music while baring all, you could make an absolute killing at naturist establishments up and down the country.

Or how about naked stand-up comedy? There has to be a whole raft of gags at the expense of the naturist community, which they will love, and if you can be funny and perform naked, you'll find plenty of work.

If you don't have any expertise or trade but would happily turn up for work in the nude, then great – you could set yourself up as a naturist window cleaner. Again, all it takes is a phone call to your local naturist club to offer your services. If they say no, you could ask if they have any openings for any other jobs, such as pool cleaner, gardener, cleaner, etc.

There is also a demand for 'life models' – people who pose nude for sketches, paintings and photographs. If you are posing for students or budding artists, the pay isn't brilliant, probably about the same as working at a bar or in a shop, but if you are posing for private photographers, the rates go up substantially. However, if you do decide to pose naked privately, ensure you take someone with you. There are some peculiar people around, so be careful.

No qualifications are required to be a life model. The only – and sometimes very difficult – skill a life model needs is to be able to keep absolutely still for long periods of time. They may also need a secondary skill – a strong bladder!

To set up as a life model requires little or no investment. Occasionally some props are required, which are normally provided by the venue. My friend, an experienced life model, keeps some seasonal props such as Santa hats and Easter bunny ears.

As a life model, there is absolutely no requirement to have a perfect body. In fact, the reverse is the case. Artists tend to love the shapes of different, diverse bodies, so they can test themselves with different angles and shading. Both male and female life models are required.

A very different area – which is regarded by many as being a risky area of enterprise – is naturist massage. You would need a spare room, a massage table, oils and hopefully some idea of how to massage. There are various courses available which would enable the masseuse or masseur to be accredited or registered with a professional body.

The idea is that you offer a massage in which the client and you are both naked. You would have to deal with the fact that a vast number of people, mostly men, expect 'something extra' at the conclusion of their massage (often known as a 'happy ending') – indeed, many naturist massage businesses do offer this.

If you want to set yourself up as a 'straight' naturist massage business, you would have to make it clear from the onset that you do not offer happy endings. Even then, be on your guard for customers who choose to ignore your rules...

I have a friend who operates as a naturist masseuse

on England's south coast, and she makes it abundantly clear from the first point of contact by her customers that she offers nothing more than a straight naturist massage. Despite this, many clients have made sexual requests of her. One guy wanted to be massaged with a nappy on, and have her remove it during the massage. (He said this wasn't a sexual desire; he had a desire to discover his inner child. Really?)

Another client deliberately undid his catheter during a massage, and spilled urine all over her massage table. He is obviously no longer a client.

On numerous occasions, she has had to leave the massage room to allow a client to 'finish himself off'. She is plagued by men phoning for an appointment who will then start making sexual requests of her.

It's not just men either! She was once approached by a woman who asked if my friend could massage her and a female friend in turn, while the other masturbated. She obviously refused. My friend still advertises her services, but does her best to be as selective as possible. Happily, she has a number of regular clients who respect her and only expect a massage with no 'extras'

I asked her if she had any advice for someone wanting to get into the same line of business, and she said: 'Decide from the beginning what you are going to offer and stick to it. If you are going to provide extras, that's up to you, but if you are going to keep it on the straight and narrow, and just offer a massage and nothing more, be blunt – to the point of rudeness, if you have to. Don't be bullied into doing anything you don't want to do.'

However, there are hundreds of naturist massage

businesses who do go to the other extreme. Instead of subtly offering a client extras, they actually advertise the fact. You only have to search online to find them!

There are many other niches within the naturist industry which are relatively unexplored: for example, how many nudist guest houses do you know of? Another Google search would provide an answer!

Most naturists have heard of Tim Higgs, who runs the successful Clover Spa Hotel in Birmingham. It is now probably the best known naturist hotel in the UK, thanks mainly to appearances on various TV shows, such as *The Hotel Inspector*. His business has caused controversy over the years, with some angry local residents demanding that his hotel be closed down. But the publicity has only served to entice more and more customers to his hotel!.

Because of the naturist slant of his business, even his application for an alcohol licence was featured in the national press.

Free publicity!

You don't have to have a hotel or guest house; you could advertise a spare room as 'nude friendly' and make some money from renting it out. There are reasonable tax allowances for home owners who rent out a room, so it could be worth your while – plus you might enjoy having like-minded lodgers.

If you are bold enough, you could be like naturists Ian and Barbara Pollard who became famous for tending their fabulous gardens at their stately home at Malmesbury, Wiltshire, in the nude. They even held open days where the general public could turn up and join in the fun.

The options are endless.

One of the latest innovative ideas for a naturist enterprise is an evening out at a restaurant where all the diners are expected to be nude. These naturist restaurants are springing up all over the world, including in Spain, Italy, France, England and America.

Hungry diners arrive at the restaurant and are invited to divest themselves of all clothing. They are then led to their table, which is normally in an area screened from other nude customers by a wicker partition or flower arrangement, to give diners a bit of intimacy and privacy, and then they are presented with the menu in the normal fashion.

In many of these restaurants, the food is fresh and organic, and the emphasis is on healthy eating.

In these restaurants, the members of staff are usually not nude, but are dressed in normal waiting attire.

Again, there is an unspoken rule that you must not sit butt-naked directly on the chairs. You will be provided with a towel, or the chair will have a removable covering that is changed before the next customer sits down. This rule applies at the vast majority of naturist establishments.

If you are going to try out a nudist restaurant, ensure that you wear a napkin on your lap to protect your bits from spills, and be careful reaching across the table for the salt – you don't want your boobs or anything else dragging through someone's meal. That could be painful – and embarrassing.

Another naturist enterprise that is proving successful is naked yoga.

Naked yoga is becoming more and more popular, together with naked Pilates. So if you are a yoga teacher and also a naturist, there is your opportunity.

Finally, in some lines of work it really doesn't matter if you are clothed or not: for example, working from home as a writer, editor, blogger, web designer, painter/artist, online model, cookery expert – in fact, you could be a real-life 'Naked Chef'!

Nude humour

According to the latest survey, women prefer undressing in front of men than in front of women. The reason is that they feel that other women are judgemental, but men are just grateful…

CHAPTER 14: NATURIST HOLIDAYS

Just like when you book a conventional holiday, before booking a naturist holiday you need to ask yourself some questions: What sort of holiday do I want? Quiet? Sociable? Camping? Boozy? And who do I want to go with?

Ah, now there's the thing. Who do I want to go with…

The people you would normally think about going on holiday with may not be the people you would want to go on a naturist holiday with, especially if it's your first time.

You might have to tell some people that you are a naturist – otherwise, imagine the look on some of your close friends or family's faces when you arrive at the naturist beach and strip off!

So your first time should ideally be with your partner or naturist friends, or even on your own if you feel brave and adventurous.

I would advise you not to tell anyone about your nudist holiday at this stage, because you may change your mind later and decide that naturism is not for you (although I doubt you will).

Then, just with any normal holiday, there are the travel-related questions: Do we drive? Do we fly? Should we just go on a naturist cruise and be done with it?

There are many options to consider, and this chapter will guide you through some of them. If you are a nervous first-time naturist and just want a relaxing beach holiday with almost guaranteed sunshine, the Canary Islands are hard to beat.

The Canaries are a group of islands off the west coast of Africa. The islands belong to Spain, and the predominant language spoken is Spanish. Because the islands are near Africa they are warm throughout the year, which makes them the ideal beach holiday destination, whether you visit during the summer or at Christmas.

Although the sun shines most of the time, there are refreshing breezes which make the heat bearable – although it's advisable to take a cardigan or light sweater for the evenings

The main islands in the Canaries are Gran Canaria, Fuerteventura, Lanzarote and Tenerife, all of which offer naturist beaches, accommodation and also complete naturist holidays.

We will take a brief look at two of the Canary Islands, Fuerteventura and Gran Canaria.

Fuerteventura

We will concentrate on the north and south of the island, as the middle part is not particularly known for its naturist activity. Corralejo is at the north and is a buzzy town offering a multitude of restaurants, cafés, high street shops and a few pubs. If you are looking for a good night out, this is the place for you. Don't worry – all ages and tastes are catered for.

The town is sizable and sits next to the sea. It offers sandy beaches, where you'll sometimes find beach sand artists displaying their work.

The beaches within Corralejo itself, are not naturist beaches. However, a short walk to the east of Corralejo reveals stretches of sands and dunes featuring man-made 'bunkers' made out of stones where naturists can get either find some privacy or gain some respite from the breezes that are a feature of the Canary Islands.

It has to be stressed here that, although the sun is tempered by the sometimes strong breeze, particularly here in Fuerteventura, you are quite near the equator so you need to be careful not to burn. As previously mentioned, take the necessary precautions, especially if you have pale skin.

As you walk away from Corralejo along the sands, with the sea to your left, you will come across a couple of similar-looking hotels. They stand out as they are the only buildings in the vicinity, and they perch on the edge of the beach. The second of these is called the Oliva Beach Hotel, and it – helpfully – is on Oliva beach.

The hotel, which is all-inclusive, is in two parts, the first of which is quite traditional. It has conventional hotel rooms, and hosts the reception area and the main restaurant. It has bar areas and an adjoining games room, and a cabaret-style bar where guests can relax and enjoy a variety of cocktails and entertainment.

The second part of the complex is more holiday chalet style, and is designed more for families and children. Both parts have individual swimming pool and bar/restaurant areas. The hotel is not a naturist hotel, but it is very popular with naturists because it sits right by a sandy beach where naturism is allowed. Here, textiles and nudists mingle in harmony with each other.

When the bar is shut, the coffee machines are left on, and there is a beer tap for those needing emergency sustenance out of hours.

Of course, if you fancy a change of scenery or a more indulgent night out, Corralejo is only a short (€5) taxi ride away.

At the Oliva Beach, there is a choice of restaurants. The main one in the hotel part of the complex seems to be the best. There, tables groan under the weight of food from all parts of the world, and you can ask for food to be cooked to order too: sometimes steak, sometimes fish; it varies. There is a pasta bar where you can mix and match pasta with different sauces, and Asian-style food.

The grounds are well kept, and in addition to the two pools there are dedicated sunbathing areas, on sand as well as grass, within the complex. Security guards look after the perimeter of the grounds to ensure that only hotel guests are permitted entry.

There are plenty of other hotels and places to stay in and around Corralejo, but the reason I recommend the Oliva Beach and the immediate area is not because I am getting any sort of back-hander from the management (hey ho...), but because it is the ideal place to start your journey into naturism.

There is no pressure to strip off straight away. The beach caters for both textiles and nudists, and the hotel itself is non-naturist, so newbies and wannabes can take their time and ease themselves into naturism, or just enjoy a conventional holiday.

This is a place where nudists can enjoy a holiday with textile friends and everyone is happy!

Getting to Oliva beach is straightforward. From Fuerteventura Airport, follow signs to Corralejo, if driving (it's just over 40 km; about a half-hour drive), or sit back in the transfer bus and enjoy the scenery as you head north.

A hotel that I haven't yet had the pleasure of visiting, but which is wholly appropriate to mention, is the Gran Hotel Natura Naturist, (www.granhotelnatura.com) to the east of Corralejo. This is a dedicated naturist hotel that boasts two swimming pools, self-catering apartments, numerous facilities, and glorious views of the Atlantic. It has a gym, a sauna, and direct access to the beach.

There are plenty of naturist-friendly beaches in Fuerteventura, and I can heartily recommend El Cotillo.

El Cotillo is to the West of Corralejo, in the north-west of the island. It has the look and feel of a small fishing village but is blessed with some excellent restaurants and lovely sandy beaches. Here, nudists and textiles can mingle freely. There are a couple of hotels nearby, but many people catch the bus from Corralejo, which goes directly to El Cotillo, or drive across.

For the more dedicated naturist, I can recommend Morro Jable which is to the south of Fuerteventura. The beaches at Morro Jable are composed of lovely soft sand and they stretch the length of the town and beyond. The main beach is known as Playa del Matorral has a mixture of nudists and textiles.

There are sun loungers with umbrellas you can hire for the day. It's useful to note that a couple of travel guides state that there are dedicated nudist areas, now I'm not sure where these 'areas' are because each time I've been there I have seen nudists *everywhere* along this beach. In fact the last time I was there I stayed at an all-inclusive complex which was not supposed to be particularly 'Naturist Friendly' but there were ladies and gentlemen completely stripped off, sunbathing side-by-side with non-naturists who clearly didn't care.

The beach sunbathing areas are contained by a netting fence which is there so you can enjoy more privacy and get a little respite from the breeze.

Inland from the main beach is a road that runs parallel to the beach, and here you will discover a selection of restaurants and bars, which should appeal to most tastes. Here also are a few hotels, a few of which are all-inclusive, or part-inclusive, so you can tailor your holiday to your budget. These are ideal for naturists, given the proximity of the beach.

Prices and standards of hotels vary, but you can get some excellent package deals online .

The mile or so of sand that stretches along the main part of Jandía is ideal for those who don't want a particularly active holiday, those who just want to lie under the hopefully blue sky, get an all-over tan, and a bit of rest.

When you get bored with sunbathing, or you want more physical activity, walk north along the beach (with the sea to your right). You can remain naked if you wish – you will see many clothed people, but don't worry, they won't take any notice as there are so many nudists around.

At the end of the beach you will see the final hotel on your left. Here the terrain changes to rock, and you will have to navigate over boulders and pebbles. When the tide is out, the walk is much easier, and you will come across a series of coves and beaches and many fellow naturists.

It is advisable to wear sandals or flip-flops as some of the rocks can be quite sharp and slippery for bare feet. There are no toilets, bars or restaurants along here so if you need a loo break, but don't want to pollute the sea, there is a little café a few hundred yards on the left.

This walk is not for the faint-hearted! Quite a few years ago I walked barefoot for miles along this stretch of beach until I came to a point where building works had caused a cliff landslide. I had two options: go back, which I was reluctant to do as I'd come so far, or go in the sea and try to swim around the pile of rocks. I couldn't walk on them because I had no shoes and the rocks were slimy and sharp.

So into the water I went. I had to swim out to sea quite a way because nearer the shore the rocks were directly under the water, making it impossible to swim. As I swam, the tide took me and carried me further out! I kept bumping into the rocks in the sea. Naturally, I was terrified, but thankfully my flailing arms finally found purchase and I was able to get back to shore with only a couple of cuts and scratches and an acute sense of embarrassment that I had been so stupid. At least there was no one else around to see me.

By now, I was at the other side of the landslide and didn't have the option of turning back, but had to carry on. After a couple of minutes back on terra firma and with the glorious sun drying my body, I quickly forgot my near-death-by-drowning experience and carried on. After a couple more miles I came across a hotel which backed onto the sea. I went through to reception and called a taxi, thanking my lucky stars that I had brought with me a bag containing shorts and a T-shirt, if no sandals!

You can keep walking for miles along this stretch. You will come across more beaches and areas of rocks, which you will have to clamber over. Watch out for the tides, though – don't get cut off, and don't be stupid and risk your life like I did!

If you are looking for remote beaches in Fuerteventura, you are in luck. Head south of Morro Jable by car, and make your way round past the south tip of the island and around to the south-west. Here you will find some remote beaches that are ideal for the shy nudist. Getting to the beaches is not always easy, so it's a good idea to take a map, but once you get there you will love the sense of privacy and solitude.

In the past, getting to these remote beaches was difficult by car because the roads were little more than dirt tracks in places, with very little passing room for oncoming vehicles, but now the roads are much better.

Gran Canaria

When I discovered the beaches of Maspalomas at the southern tip of Gran Canaria, I thought I had died and gone to heaven. Maspalomas is a Mecca for naturists, who, thanks to the climate, visit the island all year round. There are many other beaches in Gran Canaria where you can take your clothes off, but Playa de Maspalomas is one of the best. The beach stretches from Playa del Meloneras to Playa del Inglés for three or four miles.

The beach is backed by huge sand dunes – Dunas de Maspalomas, a protected nature reserve since 1897 – for which Maspalomas is famous. While hundreds of nudists sunbathe in and around the dunes, there are only a couple of enclosed 'dedicated' naturist areas, containing sun loungers and umbrellas. These can be found by walking along the beach from Meloneras, where the faro de Maspalomas (Maspalomas lighthouse) is. You can't miss it – you can see it for miles

With the sea on your right, you will pass a dedicated sunbathing area with sun loungers and a beach bar on your left, which is *not* naturist. Keep going along the beach until you come to a similar sunbathing area, again with a bar. Bingo, you have arrived.

As far as I'm aware the beach doesn't have a name but you'll know you are in the right place because of all the naked bodies!

There are no toilet facilities on this beach: however, if you walk for another two minutes you will find another nudist area, popular with gay people. This beach has clean toilets, hosted by an attendant, although there is a small charge to use the facilities.

If you go beyond the first set of dunes and look inland, you will see plenty of naked people – and some clothed – who are all clearly showing interest in something. They move around from one spot to another. Essentially they are watching people who are engaging in sexual activity (also known as 'dogging').

The dunes of Maspalomas are famous for this. The first time I visited, I remember being on the transfer bus and the tour guide mentioning 'interesting activity in the dunes', which I naively took to mean something to do with nature (which I suppose it is…). There are so many stories about the sexual goings-on in the dunes, I suspect that most of them are true. Swingers, exhibitionists and voyeurs all come together (not literally, well…) to live out their fantasies, along with couples who just want to get it on in the open air.

It took me a while to notice, however. After years of holidaying in the area, I was using the dunes as a shortcut to my hotel, having spent a pleasant day on the beach, when I saw a group of people in a thicket. I did a double-take when I saw they were naked and one of the women was kneeling down...

Now I knew what this 'interesting activity' in the dunes was all about!

The commercial part of Maspalomas

In the 1990s, this was a rocky wasteland leading to a scrappy beach with a café. Now it is a bustling area with high-end shops selling jewellery, clothes and accessories. Round the lighthouse you will find most of the cheap restaurants: these are the tourist restaurants all offering similar fare, such as pizzas, chips and burgers. If you walk beyond the lighthouse, away from the naturist beaches, you will discover some better-quality eateries. I usually prefer a burger restaurant for lunch and a better-quality restaurant for dinner, depending on the situation.

If you walk along Maspalomas beach in the other direction, just before Playa del Inglés you will come to a series of small covered restaurants, all offering great-value meals, sometimes with entertainment such as a Spanish guitarist and singer.

There is plenty to do in the evenings, depending on where you go in Gran Canaria, so do your own research first. I can recommend the famous Jumbo centre in Playa del Inglés for a night out. There are some really entertaining drag acts there that you will enjoy, whether you are gay or straight.

There are also plenty of other naturist-friendly

beaches for you to discover in other parts of Gran Canaria, and indeed in the rest of the Canary Islands, but I hope this section has given you a flavour of what is available, particularly for new nudists.

If, however, you want an all-round naturist holiday you will never forget, then Cap d'Agde is for you.

Cap d'Agde

It is almost impossible to write anything about clothes-free holidays or naturist holiday resorts without mentioning Cap d'Agde. Cap d'Agde is a naturist resort situated on the east coast of France, near Narbonne, and is famous amongst naturists worldwide. It has been described as a naturist village, since it includes restaurants, clothes shops, hairdresser, pubs, nightclubs and supermarkets, all of which are accessible to people wearing nothing.

Cap d'Agde's beach looks out over the Mediterranean and comprises beautiful golden sands. When you arrive at the resort, either on foot or by car, you are checked in through security. Once inside, it feels just unbelievable. To be able to go about your normal life naked – getting out of bed, having breakfast, sunbathing, going shopping and just wandering around – is a naturist's dream.

Imagine walking into a supermarket and seeing naked people browsing with their shopping baskets as if it is the most normal thing in the world, while being served by fully clothed staff – who have seen it all before, and then some.

There are a few areas where nudism is frowned upon within the Cap d'Agde complex – restaurants, for example, where you are expected to make at least a token gesture towards dressing-up for dinner. You

don't have to wear a suit or anything formal, just don't have your bits on show too much!

There are semi-nude people clad in basques and stockings – and don't bother making the old joke, 'And that's just the men', because here at Cap d'Agde, anything goes. There are women wearing see-through negligees or various forms of black rubber attire, and there are also people dressed comparatively normally in shirts, shorts and dresses. There are high-quality restaurants as well as less formal food outlets serving snacks and take-away food.

There are plenty of bars dotted around the complex, and the nightclubs generally attract what I would call the darker, or seedier side of naturism.

We have enjoyed many an evening sitting in a bar across from the main doors of one of the nightclubs, enjoying watching people queuing up to enter, and dressed in what looks like part of the collection of the Ann Summers catalogue.

Some people choose to forsake clothes altogether, preferring the minimalist option of absolutely nothing. I have seen a naked woman with a dog collar around her neck being led by her partner; two naked women wearing nothing but Catwoman masks, black boots and gloves; people wearing nothing but gold spray; and plenty of people in normal smart clothes.

People-watching doesn't get better or more interesting than this!

But there is also the other side. Some of the people I have met there swear they always have the best holiday ever. Some of them are totally oblivious of the extra-curricular night-time activities. As one of them put it: 'Look, the beauty of this place is that you can come here with your 90-year-old gran and grandchildren and have a wonderful naturist holiday, and you will probably never find out there is anything else going on at the village, unless of course you decide to venture out during the evening, or walk about a mile up the beach.'

He was right, I wandered along the sands about mid-afternoon, and after about ten – fifteen minutes I came across what looked like a sea of naked bodies. On closer inspection, there were dozens of nude sunbathers mixed up in overt sexual activity, observed by naked onlookers, who possibly may have been doing the same thing earlier, or who were working up to an encore!

Watching the proceedings was a man selling ice cream from his hand-cart. All this, thankfully was taking place well away from any children and families, who were much further down the beach – probably where the ice-cream seller should have been!

In some ways it seemed a bit sad and seedy. Some of the participants actually looked a bit bored and matter-of-fact as they pleasured their partners, and I kind of wondered what motivated them to want several partners in one afternoon. Would they do the same that evening? But each to their own – and at least no one was hurting anyone else, as far as I was aware.

However, overall holidaying at Cap d'Agde was one of the most entertaining, relaxing and pleasurable holidays I have ever had. It also helped that my mobile phone had no signal, so I just put it away out of site, and my holiday was entirely uninterrupted.

The apartments we stayed in were basic, but clean, and our balcony overlooked the balconies on either side, so again we were treated to an evening display of sexual entertainment, with only two couples this time. Not that we were actually looking over the balcony, you understand!

The next morning we bumped into one of the couples, and greeted them with a cheery 'Hello!'

The woman of the couple said 'Hello' back in a really posh voice, and wished us a 'wuuunderful holiday'. It just shows you, you can't label or judge people.

It didn't break the bank to stay at an apartment at Cap d'Agde, and you can also camp there, either in tents or 'glamping' style.

For the uninitiated, 'Glamping' is just posh 'camping'

There is a whole section of the site for campers and there are further camping and caravan sites outside of the village grounds for those who just want to use Cap d'Agde as a day visit.

The holiday makers at Cap d'Agde were very careful and protective of their own children, and tended also to keep an eye on other people's kids to offer the same protection.

One guy was taking a photo of his little boy swimming in the sea, and he was reprimanded by another man, who stated that the resulting photo may also include other children, and that taking photos of any sort at Cap d'Agde was considered really bad form.

I have seen heated aggression over a photo that another man was taking of the people in the sea, all in all it's very much frowned upon by everyone at Cap d'Agde. People want a relaxing holiday, not to find themselves or their family plastered all over the internet!

Bearing in mind that Cap d'Agde has a captive audience, you would expect the prices to be steep, but it wasn't. I was pleasantly surprised. In fact, there were even bargains to be had in a couple of the clothes shops.

If you want to venture out of the complex, there is a textile beach adjacent, and a few kilometres away is the town of Agde, which has a quintessential French atmosphere, and bars, cafés and wonderful markets. It's also where the nearest train station is – although many visitors to Cap d'Agde make their way to the camp by plane and are then driven to the village by one of the organisers.

I have spent more time talking about this holiday than others in this book. The reason is simple: there's more to talk about! And I think Cap d'Agde is a must for any self-respecting naturist. In fact, even if you are a non-naturist and fancy an alternative holiday, this would fit the bill!

Here we have only scratched the surface of a small selection of naturist holidays. Hopefully there should be something to suit everyone, but if not, get online; there are thousands to choose from. There's a great company called Chalfont Holidays based in Windsor in the UK (www.chalfontholidays.co.uk) who specialise in naturist holidays, and seem to have something for everyone. (No I'm not getting paid by them, they are just really good and friendly!)

As always, do your own research before you travel anywhere.

Nude humour

Two gentlemen were sitting naked, discussing political philosophy in the conservatory of their local naturist club, when one said to the other, 'Have you read Marx?'

'Yes,' replied the other, 'it's these damn wicker chairs!'

CHAPTER 15: FINDING LOVE AS A NATURIST

It can be a very difficult time for a couple when only one person wants to experiment with naturism. It can cause a divide in the relationship, and might mean that the person who wants to try naturism has to do it on their own, and sometimes might have to hide it from their partner.

I have had many conversations with men and women who fervently wish that their partner was accompanying them on their naturist journey, and that they could share this special part of their life. This doesn't necessarily mean that their partner has to become a naturist themselves, but they go together to their partner's club and join in the social experience. At my local club several couples arrive together. One will strip off and go to the pool, and the other will head to the bar, clothed. On naturist beaches around the world, it is common to see couples sunbathing where only one of the couple is totally naked.

So if you are a single person, you could be forgiven for thinking, 'Okay then, rather than having this potential problem in my life, all I need to do is meet someone who is a nudist. That way, I don't have to worry. In fact, there are bonuses – when I meet someone for a date in a pub or restaurant, I might fantasise about what they look like without their clothes. If I meet them in a naturist club, I will know what they look like without clothes, so I don't have to speculate; I can simply get on with getting to know them.'

All of this is true to a degree, but unfortunately, a relationship is unlikely to survive if it is only based on

each party being a naturist. A successful relationship is about getting on with each other and having more in common than just naturism. Trust, passion, love, shared life goals, shared experiences and being mentally attuned to each other are also essential.

Happily, some couples have met at naturist clubs or events. Some have even gone on to marry. However, this is quite rare. There are few eligible single people who frequent naturist clubs – particularly from the younger generation. The best way to find a fellow nudist companion, lover or potential spouse is to join a dedicated nudist online dating agency, such as www.nudistlovematch.com.

That way, you'll know you have at least one thing in common...

Or you could just put yourself out there and hope to bump into someone special – and, when you do, let them gently know about your naturist interests.

One of my favourites is to say, 'When I'm on holiday, I like to get a brown bum', or 'If I find myself on a nudist beach, I will strip off along with everyone else'. Both of these statements will start a conversation (in which, hopefully, the other person will either agree, or say something along the lines of, 'That's something I would like to try!'). This is far better than blurting out that you are a naturist and that you like taking your clothes off. The other person may have preconceptions about being a naturist, which will be hard to break down. Saying you like to have an all-over tan seems more acceptable to most people. I'm not sure why; it's just the way it is.

For more information about nudist dating, and finding love as a naturist, please go to the Nudist UK website.

Nude humour

There was an old man in Florida who owned a huge farm on which there was a pond. One day the farmer went down to the pond with a bucket to gather some apples from the trees next to the pond. As he drew nearer, he heard laugher and splashing. He saw a group of young women skinny dipping in his pond. Aware of his presence, the young ladies flocked to the deeper end of the pond.

One of them shouted to the farmer, 'We're naked, and we are not coming out of this pond until you leave!'

The farmer said, 'I didn't come down here to make you get out of the pond, or look at your naked bodies.' He held up his bucket. 'I came down to feed the alligator.'

Clever!

CHAPTER 16: MY FIRST TIME! TRUE NUDIST STORIES

Here are a few genuine accounts of some first experiences of naturism. I hope it helps to realise that other people have fears about shedding their clothes in public.

Teresa

I got into naturism many years ago when my children were young. My brother and his wife had tried it and raved about it, telling me that I should give it a go, so I did!

It must have been in me to be a naturist in the first place, because when the sun came out I used to spend time naked on a flat roof, but unseen by other people. So when I went to the Diogenes naturist club to become a member, my clothes came off without any hesitation whatsoever. It felt like stripping off was the most natural thing ever.

The funniest part was that the proprietor of the club shook hands as we left and said, 'I hope to see more of you.' I remember thinking, 'How much more of me is there left to see? You've seen it all!'

Now I live on a naturist club site, and would recommend naturism to anyone.

A few people I know have tried it and haven't enjoyed it, but at least they had a go. However, many, many more have tried it and have never looked back.

When I told my parents I was a naturist, they told me they wished they had done the same years ago, and my children credit their naturist upbringing to never feeling ashamed of their bodies, even when they were teenagers.

Give it a try – life is short.
Good luck!

Avril

My partner and I had started stripping off in the seclusion of his back garden during the warmer weather, and I had enjoyed being naked in the sun very much, although our movements in the garden were restricted due to being overlooked by neighbours.

So we decided to take it a stage further, and visited the Silverleigh naturist club in Kent. Initially, I was worried about what we were walking into: what sort of club it was, what sort of people went there, was there going to be any 'funny business' going on? I was also concerned about bumping into anyone I knew from the outside world.

However, the benefits were huge: it was wonderful just to be able to wander around naked without having to worry about covering up, and I particularly enjoyed being able to use the swimming pool and the lawns and grounds of the club.

I've since been to some nudist beaches. I don't like *all* nudist beaches; I hate it when you get older men parading around near the water's edge when they don't need to. But there are some great places to go, such as Eagle Peak which is a naturist resort in Spain next to Almuñécar. There I can truly relax. Wonderful.

Author's note about Almuñécar: According to their website, the proprietors have a policy of not admitting non-naturist couples. However, if one person in a couple is a naturist, then the proprietors take the view that the non-naturist can take the opportunity to try the naturist lifestyle among friendly naturists with very little pressure. Apparently they have a 100% conversion rate.

This is a superb way to get your non-naturist partner to experience naturism!

Martin

I didn't even consider nudism until I was in my late forties, when my wife and I went on a package holiday to Fuerteventura. Because there was a problem with our hotel we were told on the transfer bus that we were being upgraded to a different hotel on the south-east coast of the island.

The rooms, sea view and entertainment were great. The hotel had four or five pools and it turned out that the one furthest from the hotel and nearest to the sea was a naturist pool. Well, I say naturist pool because these naked people seemed to appear from nowhere onto a ledge and then dive into the pool.

There was a naturist sauna next to the pool that was 'skin only', although you could take your towel with you. It was the only sauna in the complex as far as I knew, and before long I was seriously contemplating stripping off and joining in.

So, plucking up some courage, I entered the sauna with the blue hotel towel that everyone else in the complex was carrying, and took a seat on one of the higher benches at the back.

The sauna was packed, and most people were totally naked, on their towels.

It was obviously hot, but it got hotter still when this German fellow with a great big moustache stood up and made a thumbs-up sign. Everyone shouted encouragement in different languages, and he threw some liquid from a vessel onto the coals.

Almost immediately there was a heady, eucalyptus smell that seared into my mouth, nostrils and lungs, making me cough but clearing everything at the same time.

The German then picked up a towel and proceeded to waft the hot air at everyone in the sauna in turn.

When he had completed his 360-degree rotation, he put down his towel and bowed, whereupon everyone in the sauna gave him a round of applause.

Then one of the other people in the sauna stood up naked and went through another door – the door that led to the swimming pool. That started everybody else, and soon everyone else went outside to cool off in the pool.

I followed, and jumped into the cool water, which gave instant relief from the sauna.

It was a completely liberating experience which faltered as I came to the edge of the pool to get out. My towel was still in the sauna, as was everyone else's, so I had to get out of the pool and walk naked along the side of the pool and up some stone stairs back to the sauna, in front of loads of people who were on their way down to the beach, all of whom were wearing swimming attire.

I was a bit embarrassed. It was one thing being naked with other naked people in the sauna, but this was the outside world with the majority of people clothed. But I kept thinking that no one would know me, although my wife would have been a bit shocked, but she was at the bar next to the main complex, quite a distance from where I was.

I got back to the sauna and loved the instant camaraderie. I had loved every second of the experience.

That night I came clean to my wife, who was quite unperturbed but also – unfortunately – unwilling to join in. She didn't like beaches, sand or swimming at the best of times.

By the end of the holiday, not only was I going for a daily sauna, but after some encouragement from my new friends I was now a regular visitor to the naturist beach. I never looked back.

My advice to anyone who is considering trying naturism is: *Please*, just try it once. Nobody will die, and you'll probably love it!

Alfred (name changed for privacy)
My first time was when I was nearly seventy (I'm eighty now). I was on holiday at Anfi Beach in Gran Canaria.

I remember we had gone to visit a place called Playa del Inglés in Gran Canaria and my mate, who is about twenty years younger than me, suggested that we walk along the beach to Maspalomas and then get a bus or taxi back to our apartment at Anfi Beach.

As we were walking along the sand it dawned on me that the people sunbathing on the beach were wearing nothing or next to nothing, and as we walked on a bit further, a crowd of completely nude people made their way into the sea right in front of us.

To my mate, I said something like, 'There's something I would like to have tried.'

He said to me, 'Listen, there's nothing stopping you now!'

I said, 'Yes, there is – fear!'

He said something about no one knowing me, and I'd never see anyone from this beach again, and I said,

'You're wrong – *you* will have seen me!'

So he said, 'Right then, we'll both strip off our shorts and run into the sea, and then back out again, and then at least you'll have done it. I can't say anything to anyone else because I will have done it with you.'

And that's exactly what happened. We reached a beach bar and grabbed a beer there, and then on the count of three we dropped our shorts and ran out into the sea.

I can honestly say that it was one of the most pleasurable experiences of my life. The feeling of swimming naked was amazing.

Afterwards, when we were back at the beach bar with our shorts on, I warned my mate to never breathe a word to anyone about our experience.

I have often thought of that day. It's a happy memory. I wish I'd started being a naturist when I was very much younger, I loved it so much.

My mate was as good as his word – he told no one. But after a few years, I started telling anyone and everyone. I thought, sod it, I've done nothing wrong and in fact I'm proud of it.

My little adventure probably doesn't sound much, but it was a big deal to me at the time.

Helen

I went on a naturist camping holiday in Western France. It was nothing like I expected.

The only reason I agreed to go was because one drunken night my husband and I had agreed to do it as part of a sort of 'bucket list'. When it came around to holiday booking time, my husband gleefully showed me a load of naturist-only options.

We eventually plumped for camping because funds were low, and I'm so pleased we did because we spent the entire week naked. Try to imagine getting out of bed (well, a sort of sleeping bag arrangement) naked, cooking naked, going down to the river to swim naked, etc.

There was no embarrassment whatsoever because everyone else was nude as well.

There was a bit of socialising: we did the camp fire bit, again naked, and played nude tennis, pétanque and a form of rounders with other people at the camp. It was like being in a different world: nobody cared about anybody else being naked. Young, old, middle-aged – no one cared. I loved it.

When we got back home I actually resented having to put clothes on. Weirdly, they felt constricting after that wonderful week of total freedom.

Nude humour

'I like to grab a cup of tea, sit down and then do my online shopping in the nude.
The only problem is that I keep getting told to leave by the owner of the internet café!'

CHAPTER 17: OLDER NATURISTS

Naturism is definitely seen as something that older people do. This is despite news coverage of younger people being involved in various naked activities such as nudist rallies, bike rides, protests and so forth, together with television programmes such as *My Daughter, the Teenage Nudist*. I think this is because younger people are more reluctant to be labelled, and also less inclined to be involved in *any* organisation, let alone a naturist one. This seeming imbalance has led to cries from older members: 'We need younger blood in our clubs to maintain the membership!' But many younger people who attend naturist clubs do so because they were introduced by their parents or other family members. Even then, at a certain age they disappear from the scene to pursue new interests. Sometimes they return later on in life.

So why is naturism so much more attractive to older people?

Sometimes, people decide to throw caution to the winds and do the things they haven't done so far. You'll read of 90-year-olds bungee-jumping or sky-diving, or running their first marathon – before it's too late.

For many people, naturism is one of those activities.

When I interviewed some older members from various clubs and asked how they got involved in naturism, I found that many people, who were well into their eighties, had become naturists when they were middle-aged – and had discovered they loved it. In fact, most members had found their way into naturism at an advanced age, and only some had been introduced to it earlier in life.

So my question is not 'Why aren't there more young naturists out there?' but 'Why aren't there more *older* naturists out there?'

When you visit any naturist beach or club you'll always see groups of naturists who are middle-aged and older, swimming, socialising, enjoying themselves, laughing, befriending new people, chatting, relaxing, and looking fit and tanned.

I know naturism isn't for everyone, and I respect that, but in recent years it has been widely reported that there is a worldwide problem with older people being lonely and miserable. Perhaps naturism could be a way forward!

There are some older naturists who regularly use the clubhouse pool during the summer, and will continue socialising throughout the year, attending theme nights, participating in pool and darts competitions, quizzes, celebrations and annual events. Now, these are clothed events. You don't have to be naked all of the time at a naturist club; I don't know anybody who is. Most people are naked in the pool or on the poolside, or in the gardens and on the patio, but that is generally only when the sun shines.

Common sense prevails. If it's a cold day, most people will keep their clothes on.

Similarly, most people using the clubhouse – at any time of year – will be clothed. There may be theme nights where little is left to the imagination, but even then some people still dress conventionally. That's the beauty of naturism – nobody judges!

I know a family of five, comprising two parents and three children, who regularly attend the clubhouse. The parents never go near the swimming pool but spend their afternoons playing pool in the clubhouse, naked. Nobody judges them, nobody cares. They are having a good time and that's that.

I also know of people who attend the clubhouse and never get naked. There is a gentleman who comes with his naturist wife. While she is swimming and sunbathing, he is supping a pint at the clubhouse bar, fully clothed, and chatting with the other members.

Everybody, young and old, should at least visit their local naturist club to see what they are missing. Some naturist clubs have open days where anyone can attend, but usually people just ring the club and ask for a day visit. You'll be shown around the club and the grounds and will be made to feel very welcome.

So if you looking for something to spice up your life, and want to meet new friends, become healthier, fitter and possibly increase your life expectancy, naturism could be an answer – however old you are.

However, you would be welcome in to naturism at any age.

As previously mentioned, most naturist clubs have fantastic facilities: tennis, boules, badminton, swimming pools (sometimes indoor as well as outdoor), pool tables, table tennis, saunas and more, all designed to keep you fit. If you think about how much a gym membership is, and compare it to the annual fee that most naturist clubs charge (usually around £100–£230), and then factor in all the free social events, the lovely grounds, the swimming pool and the warm community spirit of most clubs, then the annual fee looks very cheap indeed.

Also, at most clubs the food and drinks are well below pub prices, and there are sometimes cheaper 'specials' on offer – doesn't that encourage you to become a member?

The other thing that happens is that you make friends at the club, and then become part of their social group, and you will find yourself getting invited to their parties or gatherings.

Bear in mind that communal centres such as pubs and social clubs are very much on the decrease, so it is getting harder to find ways of meeting and interacting with other people, hence the popularity of Facebook and other social networking sites.

You may also find yourself invited on holiday with other club members. Most of us have been to all sorts of amazing places, where naturism is either allowed or encouraged, purely because a friend from the club has either invited us or recommended somewhere. There is no way that we would have considered those places just by going online, despite review sites such as Trip Advisor. You can't beat a review from a real live person!

I mentioned some of these places in previous chapters.

Naturism does cross age boundaries. Please don't think that all 'oldies' are lumped together. Far from it. The common interest is naturism, and it transcends age, creed, sex, religion or race. When you find yourself at a naturist social event, look around. You will observe a healthy mix of all types of people, conversing, socialising, and having fun.

Equally, if you feel more comfortable talking to your own age or peer group, nobody will judge you.

If you are nervous at the thought of sticking a toe into naked territory, please don't worry. The first thing to do is become more confident. Not everyone can just waltz into their local naturist club, or onto the nudist beach, and immediately feel comfortable. Most people have to work up to the idea, and there are many ways of doing this.

Going on a nudist holiday has already been mentioned, and is an excellent idea providing you have made up your mind to become a naturist (at least for the duration of the holiday). If you haven't made up your mind, then it's bit of a baptism of fire to go and find yourself surrounded by boobs, bums and willies!

There are easier ways. A day visit at your local club is great, but if you want to experience being naked in front of others for just a few seconds, finding a naturist swim could be just the ticket.

Google 'naturist swim' to find your nearest. Also try http://greatbritishskinnydip.co.uk/

Many swimming pools in the country host a nudist swim on a weekly or monthly basis. There's normally a small charge, and the likelihood of meeting anyone you know is minimal. Most nude swims are in the evenings.

Arrive at the pool with a best friend – your towel. This is your backup and your comfort blanket. Once you have shed your street clothes in the changing room, step out into the pool area and take a deep breath.

How does that feel? Not so bad, is it? The fact that everyone is naked may make you feel 'one of the crowd' – or maybe you feel like running for the hills? If so, you have your towel. Go to the edge of the pool and slide into the water. You are now pretty much invisible to others.

Enjoy the swim. I can almost guarantee that you will forget about other people and will focus on swimming and the sensation of the water against your bare skin. Afterwards, when you have showered, dressed and are making your way home, replay the events in your mind. Was it that dreadful?

Welcome to naturism. I bet you wish you had done it years ago!

Nude humour

A man with a clipboard was going around a neighbourhood collecting census information. At one house he came to, the door was open by a totally naked woman.

'Don't worry,' she said, 'I'm a nudist.'

Although he was embarrassed, the man asked the first question from his clipboard. 'How many children do you have?'

'Nineteen,' she replied.

'Nineteen children?' he exclaimed. 'No wonder you're a nudist – you haven't had time to get dressed!'

CHAPTER 18: YOUNGER NATURISTS

Some time ago, I watched a TV programme which looked at naturism in the UK and featured the Fiveacres Club in Hertfordshire. By all accounts, when the film people were at Fiveacres making the documentary, they were charming and seemed genuinely interested in all aspects of naturism.

When the programme was aired, I found it to be sneery, out of touch and a bit damning of older nudists. It had the feel of the old clichéd postcards depicting a nudist barbecue with the punchline 'Careful pricking the sausages!'

The second part of the programme extolled the idea that young nudists want something different (true) and showed a group of teenage-plus naturists, together with the programme presenter, walking through a wood, stripping off by a lake (I think the presenter kept his shorts on) and then jumped into the water – ignoring the old bicycle wheels, shopping trolleys and other sharp objects in the lake (and never mind the mud, animal poo and anything else dangerous that the lake had to offer).

How irresponsible is that? -Or am I just showing my age?

For goodness sake if you are going to swim in a lake in Great Britain that already shows signs of immersed junk, please take care!

It is interesting watching the journey of a younger person involved in naturism. When a couple start to bring their children to the club, at first the kids love it. They're in and out the pool, running around very happily and usually well behaved too. In their mid-teens, though, an understandable change in attitude happens. The girls become more self-conscious: they will come to the edge of the pool wrapped in a towel and then slide into the water, and then reverse the process when they come out. Their visits to the club with their parents become less and less frequent, then they completely stop. Boys, on the other hand, tend not to mind others seeing them naked, but again, during their teenage years, they too will disappear to pursue their own interests.

Years later, they may return to the naturist scene with their own young families, and the cycle will start again. But this does mean there is a shortage of younger people coming into naturism. Many people think that naturist clubs are full of 'old wrinklies', which is sort of true, but on a sunny weekday you will obviously encounter more older naturists at a club because younger people of are presumably working. Go to a naturist club at the weekend or to a social event in the evening, and you will find younger people.

The answer to 'how can we get more younger people involved in naturism?' is 'I don't know'. People in their twenties are normally trying to build a career and bring up a family. Relaxing in the sun is reserved for holidays – if they can afford them.

Interestingly, when you do encounter younger naturists on a beach on holiday, they seem to have a very different concept of naturism; older naturists tend to sunbathe either as a group or in pairs, and their solo counterparts will either latch onto a group or discreetly tuck themselves away.

On naturist-friendly sunny beaches, particularly in the Canaries and the Balearic islands, I have often seen a group of teenagers wearing costumes, and one of the females or males in the group will be totally nude. This is naturist integration at its best. None of the other members of the group seems to care that a friend is naked; they just sit, talking and laughing together. I love this. It's even healthier in some ways than wholesale naturism, because each member of the group is doing what they want to do with total respect for their peers, and with no sexual agenda.

So while it would be nice to have a healthy balance of all ages and both sexes involved in naturism, the fact that fewer young people seem interested in naturism doesn't mean that it will die out. It will never die out. It has been around forever, and – depending on the social climate – will come and go and then re-emerge as fashions and attitudes change.

I think that there is very little incentive for people in their late teens and early twenties to attend and become a member of a naturist club. The joining fee is somewhere between £120 to £250 per annum, depending on location and facilities. This is prohibitive to a younger person, who will not want to plan their summer activities but just take things on a day by day basis. So they are more likely to attend their local club on a day visitor basis, which costs around £10–£20.

In most clubs, evening social events are strictly for members only, which of course prevents day visitors from attending, so there is no way they can integrate and become part of the club.

What's the answer? Maybe a vastly reduced membership fee for people aged under 25, or for students? This would at least incentivise them to join, attend the club more frequently, and join in with social activities, leading to a win–win situation for all – and a younger naturist element coming through the ranks. Come on, you naturist clubs, try it out! It'll cost you nothing in real terms, but you may get some new members.

Nude humour

Always swim nude – sharks hate to peel their food!

CHAPTER 19: PUBLIC NUDITY

Being a naturist doesn't mean you can be naked at official naturist places such as the beach or club; there are plenty of organised nude activities as well, including nude swims at your local swimming pool (check first; don't just turn up and strip off!) or organised nude swims at a beach or a lake. Sometimes there are other outdoor activities which are slightly more niche, such as naked gardening or naked rambling.

Now, you would expect to see some exposed flesh at a beach or a lake, and naked gardening would be behind a garden wall, but naked rambling carries a risk. Ramblers will wander through woodlands, fields, hills and dales, naked except for backpacks and walking boots or shoes. When they see someone in the distance they will quickly don some clothing such as shorts and T-shirt. When the other person is out of sight they resume their naked journey.

The benefits of naked rambling are (1) healthy exercise and (2) the feel of the wind and sun against your bare skin and (3) the camaraderie of being with like-minded souls. The downside of naked rambling is being seen by someone who may be offended – which of course could be anyone.

Being naked in public is in itself not a crime: however, it is all about context. If you are naked in your back garden, which is not overlooked, where your nudity cannot possibly cause any offence to others, then there should be no problem. On an unofficial nudist beach (that is, a beach that is commonly recognised to accept nudity), you are unlikely to have any problems. If, however, someone decides they are offended by your nudity and asks you to cover up, it's probably a good idea to do so.

It is part of naturism to accept and embrace differences – not just bodily differences, but differences in people's opinions and attitudes – so respect for others' views is essential. It's also common sense.

When sunbathing on many unofficial nude beaches in Wales, such as the one near Kenfig, you can see people far in the distance coming towards you, which gives you a chance to grab a towel or a shirt.

Local dog walkers and people are fully aware that there is nude sunbathing going on, but out of sheer respect, we all cover up any potentially offending parts of our anatomy and wish that person a good day or wave a cheery hello. Passers-by probably think we are a bunch of friendly nutters, but it doesn't matter, no one is offended, and we can resume our sunbathing session when they have gone.

With naturist rambling, however, the situation is a bit different. When you are walking along a beach you expect to find people in a state of undress or showing some bare flesh, but when you are out for a stroll in the country, the last thing you expect to see is a group of naked ramblers. The naked ramblers will probably apologise and cover up, but some of the people who have accidentally stumbled on the ramblers may feel offended, and may report the ramblers to the authorities.

The most famous naked rambler is probably Stephen Gough, who has spent nine years in prison thanks to pursuing his 'hobby'. Stephen is primarily an activist and protester, his main protest being the right to be naked, although many would argue that they have a right *not* to see him naked.

He famously walked in the buff from Land's End to John O'Groats, and has done much to draw attention to some of the absurdity of the UK's laws, restrictions and attitudes, simply by the amount of press coverage that has been generated.

The law says that, while it isn't illegal to go naked in public, it is, however an offence to expose one's genitals with the intent of causing someone 'alarm or distress' (according to section 66 of the Sexual Offences Act 2003). Mr Gough, according to reports, has not intended to cause any alarm or distress, so you may have a degree of sympathy for his crusade. However, that sympathy may be diminished by the fact that Mr Gough shed his clothes during a flight between Southampton and Edinburgh, for which he was imprisoned for seven months. It is one thing to feel you have the right to be naked in certain circumstances, but it is quite another to force your views on people on an aeroplane where no one has the option to ignore a fellow passenger's nudity or leave the plane. Most importantly, there were children on that flight. While I condone family nudity in the appropriate surroundings and circumstances, people should have a choice over what they want to look at, and what they want their children to look at. Taking your clothes off in a confined space such as a plane, forces one's nudity onto other people, taking away their choice. If you see nudity on TV, you have the option to change channel or switch off. On a flight, confronted with a naked person, there isn't that option.

I think we should have respect for all other people, and I believe that Steven Gough made a serious misjudgement in this instance – a misjudgement that may have detracted from his own credibility. What he has succeeded in doing overall however, is at least bringing the subject of naturism to people's attention.

Other countries seem to have a very different attitude towards public nudity. Until 2011, public nudity was actively encouraged in Barcelona, Spain. It is amazing to think that it was lawful to travel naked by bus or Metro, and wander nude around the streets and parks of the city. However, this changed in 2011, when a law was passed prohibiting nudity – or even wearing a swimming costume – in the street. Now, you can be fined for being in a state of undress. The good news, however, is that many of Barcelona's beaches are nude-friendly, and you can go topless on any of the beaches.

In 2014 in Munich, Germany, nudists rejoiced at the news that the law had changed to allow them to pursue their favourite hobby. It was now okay to appear naked in public. Today, sun worshippers in Munich can legally strip off in six clothes-free zones across the city.

Oregon in the USA has lenient laws that allow nudity in some public places, providing it has no sexual undertones. But before you book your flight across the Atlantic, do some research and find out which areas and forests allow naked rambling, or where you can definitely shed your clothes, because the local laws are ambiguous.

However, in Denmark there is no such ambiguity. The human body holds little mystery for Danes, many of whom enjoy swimming naked in the country's many lakes and pools. They are taught from an early age that there is no shame in nakedness, and this is reflected in their attitude towards life. For example, there is no privacy in communal swimming pool changing rooms, where people are expected to shower, naked, before entering the pool.

If you wanted to live your life completely naked all the time, this would be nigh on impossible anywhere in the world. Yes, there are places such as Cap d'Agde where you can spend a limited amount of time naked, a few weeks or months, perhaps, and you can buy a property on-site and go shopping naked, but what happens when you want to buy a new car, for example? Naturist car showrooms are probably a long way off...

What about if you have to have your car serviced, or repaired? What about if you wanted to see a film or watch a play?

Or if you fancy a trip to McDonald's? – Or any other fast food outlet. I won't make any stupid jokes about going into Burger King and asking for a Whopper... Uh-oh, too late!

Nude humour

An old lady phoned 999 and said, 'I need the fire brigade to come quickly. There are two naked men climbing up towards my bedroom window!'

'It's the police you need,' said the operator.

The old woman yelled, 'No! The fire brigade! -they need a longer ladder!'

CHAPTER 20: AND FINALLY...

After this chapter I have included a directory of naturist clubs in the UK – use it to find your local club or to look up new clubs.

I wanted to finish the book by saying that I sincerely hope that this book has given you plenty to think about, and also taught you something about naturism.

Naturism is not a perversion; it is the simple act of enjoying life (or part of it) without clothes and experiencing all the wonderful sensations that result.

However, it is almost impossible to describe the benefits of naturism in words alone. It is something you have to experience for yourself, even if it's only once.

Bear in mind that dependant on your beliefs, you only have one life on this earth. Make the most of it, and don't miss out on any of the positive experiences that come along.

Nude *humour*

A man and his wife were at an art exhibition, where they saw a picture of a beautiful naked woman, her private parts covered with leaves.

The woman didn't like the painting and moved on, but her husband kept looking at it.

'What are you waiting for?' she asked.

'Autumn,' he replied.

NATURIST CLUBS IN THE UK

If your club isn't listed here, or is incorrectly listed, email us and if possible we will correct the information in a future updated edition: sandy@howtobeanaturist.com

Naturist clubs by county

Bedfordshire
Blackthorns Sun Club
Risely Road
Sharnbrook
Bedfordshire MK44 1NE
01234 782212
New membership enquiries: 07974 303151
www.blackthorns.org.uk

Facilities
Outdoor pool, sauna, lawns, snack bar, children's play area, clubhouse, badminton, mini-tennis, volleyball, social events.

Berkshire
Crowthorne Heritage Club
Heath Ride
Finchampstead
Crowthorne
Berkshire RG45 6BS
01344 775032
www.heritageclub.org

Facilities
Camping facilities and caravan spaces with hook-ups.

Themed social nights, outdoor pool, sauna, clubhouse, youth hut with TV, PlayStation and table football.

Buckinghamshire
Diogenes Sun Club
Chalfont St Peter
Slough
Bucks SL9 0RD
01494 857602
www.diogenessunclub.co.uk
publicity@diogenessunclub.co.uk

Facilities
Set in 6 acres of landscaped grounds. Space for motorhomes, tents and caravans. Large heated outdoor pool, sun lawn, children's play area, sauna, plunge pool, showers, heated indoor pool, lounge.

Cambridgeshire
Cambridge Outdoor Club
The Orchard, The Borough
Aldreth CB6 3PJ
01353 741335
www.cambridgeoutdoorclub.org
membership@cambridgeoutdoorclub.org

Facilities
Clubhouse with wood-burning stove, kitchen, small shop, sauna, sun room, free internet, swimming pool, children's area, camping facilities, electric hook-ups for caravans and motor homes, boules, barbeque.

Croft Country Club
Greenend
Off Halfpenny Toll Road
Three Holes
Wisbech PE14 9JD
01354 638445
www.croftcountryclub.co.uk
bookings@croftcountryclub.co.uk

Facilities
Log cabins and a camping hut for hire, plus hook-ups for caravans. Outdoor pool, indoor pool, clubhouse, sauna suite, pétanque, bowls, mini-tennis, shuffleboard court, 18-hole putting green.

Cheshire
Manchester Sun and Air Society
Springfield
Sandy Lane
Middlewich Road
Lower Peover
Knutsford WA16 9JF
07757 084046 or
07821 805866
www.springfieldmsas.org
msawarden@hotmail.com

Facilities
Heated outdoor pool, clubhouse, sauna, children's play area, mini-tennis, pétanque, cosy TV lounge, bowls.

North Western Sunbathing Society
Macclesfield

Cheshire
07787-115313
www.hillside-nwss.16mb.com
membsecnwss@mail.com

Facilities
Pavilion with kitchen and gas cooker, five acres of mature woodland, sunbathing lawns, fishpond, ornamental gardens, timber terrace, Swedish style sauna, boules, woodland walks, bring and share buffets, situated on the edge of the Peak District National Park.

Cornwall
St Columb Major
Cornwall TR9 6HY
01637 880938
www.southleigh-manor.com

Facilities
Log cabins and static caravans for hire. Camping. Outdoor pool, Jacuzzi, children's play area, paddling pool, boules, sunbathing areas, licensed bar and bistro, sauna, sun beds.

Cumbria
The Solway Club
Junction 44 of M6
Carlisle, Cumbria
01228 529764
07943 496100
www.solwaysunclub.com
Solwaysunclub@Yahoo.com

Facilities
Set in 15 acres of woodland. Campsite and facilities
for camper vans and static caravans. Clubhouse,
swimming pool, shower block, sunbathing lawn,
pétanque, volleyball, pool table, Wi-Fi, rental caravan,
sauna

Lakeland Outdoor Farm
Stoup Dub Farm
Haverigg
Millom
Cumbria LA18 4ES
01484 863036
www.lakelandoutdoorclub.co.uk
marion@lakelandoutdoorclub.co.uk

Facilities
Space for camping and caravanning. Located next to a
quiet beach.

Devon
Acorns Naturist Retreat
Creacombe Parsonage Farm
Rackenford
Tiverton
Devon EX16 8EL
01884 881260
www.acornsindevon.co.uk
andy@acornsindevon.co.uk

Facilities
Set in 13 acres of land, with spaces and facilities for
mobile homes, camper vans, caravans and tents.
Swimming pool, hot tub, sauna, pool table, Wi-Fi,

naturist bed and breakfast, activity days, Swedish massage, licensed bar. Nearby naturist beaches include Budleigh Salterton, Weston Mouth, Sillery Sands, Wild Pear beach and Saunton Sands.

Dorset
Avondale Sun Club
Highwood Copse
New Forest
Verwood
Dorset BH31 6EJ
01202 821362

Facilities
Set in 4.5 acres of woodland. Swimming pool, kids' clubhouse and play area, sauna, changing rooms, table tennis, mini-tennis, boules.

Rivendell
Horton Heath
Wimbourne
Dorset BH21 7JN
01202 083417
www.rivendelloutdoorclubltd.co.uk

Facilities
Extensive grounds with outdoor pool, mini-tennis, badminton, hot tub, sauna.

Bournemouth and District Outdoor Club
Matchams
Ringwood
Dorset BH24 2BU
07775 968518

www.bdoc.co.uk
bdocnat@hotmail.co.uk

Facilities
Situated on the edge of the New Forest near Studland naturist beach. Heated pool, sun terrace, sauna, boules, table tennis, pool table, social nights.

South Western Outdoor Club
Near Batcombe
Dorchester
Dorset
07534 091443
www.swoc-naturist.co.uk
secretary@swoc-naturist.co.uk

Facilities
Set in an area of Outstanding Natural Beauty near Studland Bay. Clubhouse, mini-tennis, pétanque.

Durham
Greenacres Sun Club
Old Alms Houses
Steadmans Lane
Cornsay Village
Durham DE7 9EH
07538 656029
www.greenacresclub.org.uk
greenacresclub@yahoo.co.uk

Facilities
Space for camping and trailer tents, and electric hook-ups. Clubhouse with licensed bar, patio, barbeque area, swimming pool, volleyball, mini-tennis,

badminton, sheltered lawns.

Essex
Arcadians of Greenglades
Greenglades
Blind Lane
Billericay
Essex CM12 9SN
07813 346631
www.greenglades.org
linda@greenglades.org
pat@greenglades.org

Facilities
Set in woodland with an area for tents. Clubhouse, pavilion, heated swimming pool, sunbathing lawns, sauna, children's playground, mini-tennis, snooker/pool, table tennis, boules.

Oakwood Sun Club
Near Noak Hill
Romford
Essex RM3 7NA
07960 109041
www.oakwoodsunclub.co.uk
bobatoakwood@yahoo.co.uk

Facilities
Set in 5.5 acres of woodland with walks. Outdoor pool, lawn, children's play area, patio, clubhouse, pool table.

Springwood Sun Club
Cooks Hall Road

West Bergholt
Essex CO6 3EY
07889 044072
www.springwoodsunclub.co.uk (contact via the
website please).

Facilities
Set in 7 acres of woodland. Clubhouse, pavilion,
heated outdoor pool, big film screen, pétanque, mini-
tennis, sun lawn, table tennis.

Gloucestershire
Tara Club
Mapleridge Lane
Chipping Sodbury
South Gloucester BS37 6PB
01454 294256

Facilities
Spaces for caravans, tents and tourers. Swimming
pool, lawns, patio area, woodland walks. Holds sports
and social events.

Pines Outdoor Club
Glasshouse Hill
Longhope
07554 543841
www.pinesoutdoorclub.org.uk
pines_sec@live.co.uk

Facilities
Set in 8 acres of lawns and woodland. Sun lawns,
nature observation.
Hampshire

Haslemere Sun Club
Sunnyacres
Pond Road
Headley Down
Bordon GU35 8NN
01428 712204
07909 902568
www.sunnyacres.co.uk
memsec@sunnyacres.co.uk

Facilities
Members' cabins and camping in a woodland setting. Sunbathing lawns, pavilion, outdoor heated pool, volleyball, badminton, pétanque, children's pool.

Hertfordshire
Fiveacres Country Club
Junction 21a of M25
Bricket Wood
St Albans AL2 3PY
01923 673073
www.fiveacrescountryclub.com
info@fiveacrescountryclub.com

Facilities
Set in 7 acres of sunbathing lawns. Camping facilities. Clubhouse with licensed bar and eatery, sun terrace, heated outdoor pool, children's play area, pétanque, mini-tennis. Runs plenty of social events.

Sunfolk Society
The Spinney
Hazel Road
Park Street

St Albans AL2 2AJ
01727 873576
www.sun-folk.org.uk
info@sun-folk.org.uk

Facilities
Set in 5 acres of woodland. Clubhouse with wood-burning stoves, outdoor heated pool, sauna, snooker, pool, table tennis, conservatory.

Spielplatz Naturist Club
Lye Lane
St Albans AL2 3TD
(If you're using a sat-nav, use postcode AL2 3TE)
01923 672126
www.spielplatz.club

Facilities
Set in 11 acres of grounds with footpaths. Clubhouse with restaurant and licensed bar, outdoor pool, solarium, hot tub, pool table, fitness equipment and children's play area. Holds social events.

Isle of Wight
Valerian Sun Club
Havenstreet
Ryde, Isle of Wight
www.valeriansunclub.com
valeriansunclub@hotmail.com

Facilities
Set in natural woodland with spaces for tents and caravans. Clubhouse, conservatory, barbeque, table tennis, boules, pétanque.

Kent
Eureka Naturist Club
Manor Lane
Fawkham DA3 8ND
01474 704418
www.eureka-naturist-club.co.uk

Facilities
Set in 23 acres of lawns, fields and woodlands. On-site accommodation available. Outdoor heated pool, clubhouse, Jacuzzis, steam room, sauna. Holds social events.

The Naturist Foundation
Sheepcote Lane
Orpington BR5 4ET
Gate is marked 'Brocken Hurst'
01689 871200
www.naturistfoundation.org

Facilities
Camping meadow. Heated swimming pool, pavilion with sun terrace, sauna, children's play area, licensed bar, café, mini-tennis, volleyball, pétanque, badminton, table tennis, outdoor gym.

Silverleigh
London Road
West Kingsdown

Kent TN15 6EX
01474 853438
www.silverleigh.com
info@silverleigh.com

Facilities
Large gardens, hotel room facilities, café and restaurant. Indoor pool, Jacuzzi and spa baths, Turkish steam room, Swedish sauna cabin, table tennis.

Lancashire
Lancashire Sun Naturist Club
Hazel Grove
Sandy Lane
Rufford
Ormskirk L40 1SX
01704 853438
www.lancashiresun.org.uk
secretary@lancashiresun.org.uk

Facilities
Set in 10 acres of grounds with woodland and facilities for camping, camper vans and tourer caravans. Sunbathing area, clubhouse, open-air solar-heated pool, sauna, mini-tennis.

Norfolk
Broadland Sun Association
31 Brickle Road
Stoke Holy Cross
Norfolk NR14 8NG
07823 405582
www.broadlandsun.co.uk

info@broadlandsun.co.uk

Facilities
Set in 25 acres, with woodland and a fishing lake. Touring caravan and tent camping areas, and electric hook-ups for caravans. Heated swimming pool, clubhouse, sauna, badminton, pétanque, mini-tennis.

Abbots Farm Naturist Site
Mill Road
North Tuddenham
near Dereham
Norfolk NR20 3DD
01362 858871

Facilities
Area for caravans, campers and tents. Indoor pool.

Nottinghamshire
Nottingham Sun Club
Brackenwood
Papplewick Road
Hucknall NG15 8GD
www.nottssunclub.co.uk
membership.sec@hotmail.co.uk

Facilities
Swimming pool, bowling green, large pavilion, small library, children's facilities, tennis court, sauna, pool table, hot tub, darts, mini-tennis, volleyball.

Oxfordshire
OxNat (Oxford Naturist Club)
07941 435021

www.oxnat.org.uk
membership@oxnat.org.uk

Facilities
Set in 12 acres of woodland. Lawns, clubhouse, sauna, kitchen, hot tub, pool, table tennis.

Shropshire
Telford Naturist Club
The Windings
Grange Lane
Telford TF2 9PB
01952 610873
www.telfordnaturistclub.com
info@telfordnaturistclub.com

Facilities
Set in 23 acres of woodland. Caravan and camping pitches, clubhouse with licensed bar, heated outdoor swimming pool, entertainment, sauna.

Somerset
Ridgewood Sun Club
Clevedon
Somerset BS23
07909 641103
www.ridgewoodsunclub.co.uk
secretary@ridgewoodsunclub.co.uk

Facilities
Camping. Clubhouse, splash pool, trampoline, barbeque, boules, mini-tennis.
Surrey
The Whitehouse Club

10 Southview Road
Warlingham
Surrey CR6 9JE
07952 788377
www.whitehouseclub.org.uk
info@whitehouseclub.org.uk

Facilities
Accommodation. Clubhouse with licensed bar, large swimming pool, small pool, sauna, two tennis courts, sauna, mini-tennis, table tennis, badminton, volleyball, boules, children's play area, conservatory.

Sussex
Apollo Sun Club
The Weild
Langton Lane
Hassocks
BN6 9EZ
07754 390535
Apollosunclub.co.uk

Facilities
Chalets and tent pitches to hire. Heated swimming pool, clubhouse, sauna, sun lawns, mini-tennis, boules, putting, table tennis, snooker.

Bristol Gardens Health Spa
24–26 Bristol Gardens
Kemptown
Brighton BN2 5JR
01273 698904

Facilities

Hot tubs, massage room, cold plunge shower, television room, swimming pool, solarium, library, refreshment lounge, Jacuzzi, saunas, vertical tanning unit.

Yorkshire
Ashdene Naturist Club
500 Elland Road
Halifax HX5 9JB
07519 952807
https://ashdene.club
visitors@ashdene.club

Facilities
Set in 7 acres of south-facing land. Camping field and caravans to rent. Clubhouse, heated outdoor pool, sauna, sun lawn, mini-tennis, pétanque, catering kitchen, licensed bar, conservatory.

The White Rose Club
Ashwood
Cross Lane
Flaxton YO60 7QZ
07743 868809
www.whiteroseclub.com
whiteroseclub@hotmail.co.uk

Facilities
Woodland. Camping. Clubhouse, bar, sauna, rental caravans, heated swimming pool, children's play area, mini-tennis, boules, lawn darts, barbeque.
Yorkshire Sun Society
Carlum Lane
Cumbria Way

Hull HU7 5YX
07501 174108
www.yorkshiresun.co.uk
info@yorkshiresun.com

Facilities
Set in 26 acres of woodland. Caravan hook-ups and camping facilities. Clubhouse with licensed bar and kitchen, swimming pool, Jacuzzi, sauna, mini-tennis, pétanque, sun lawn, barbeque.

SCOTLAND
Scottish Outdoor Club
Inchmurrin Island
Loch Lomond
Balmaha, Glasgow
G63 0JY
West Dumbartonshire

Facilities
Clubhouse, sauna, mini-tennis, huge swimming pool (the loch!).

Sunnybroom Club
Corennie Wood
near Alford
Aberdeen
07794 711627
www.nakedscotland.org.uk/clubs/sunnybroom
sunnybroom@hotmail.com

Facilities
Camping, caravans, tents. Clubhouse with kitchen and log burner, sauna, boules court, swimming nearby.

WALES
Tything Barn Naturist Campsite
West Williamston, Kilgetty
Pembrokeshire SA68 0TN
01646 651452
www.tything-barn.co.uk
info@tything-barn.co.uk

Facilities
Set in 23 acres of woodland, lawns and lagoons. Chalet and cottage rental, pitches for touring caravans. Near the sea.

Valley of Glamorgan Sun Club (now known as Woodpeckers in Wales)
www.woodpeckers-in-wales.co.uk

Facilities
Set in 5 acres of wooded countryside. Clubhouse, heated indoor swimming pool, kitchen, conservatory, sunbathing lawns, shuffleboard, boules, pool table, social events (bingo, dancing, karaoke).

Western Sunfolk
c/o Croes Roberts Farm Bungalow
Llanishen Far Wood
Trellech NP25 4PJ
07972 385428
www.westernsunfolk.org.uk
enquiries@westernsunfolk.org.uk

Facilities
Large clubhouse with kitchen, lounge and TV. Large,

covered heated swimming pool, sunbathing lawns, children's play area, mini-tennis, boules, pool table, darts, table tennis.

NATURIST ASSOCIATIONS

The International Federation of Naturism
www.inf-fni.org

British Naturism
01604 620361
www.bn.org.uk

Irish Naturist Association (INA)
PO Box 1077
Churchtown
Dublin 14
00 353 86 8370395
www.irishnaturism.org

Scottish Naturism
www.nakedscotland.org.uk

Nudist UK
www.NudistUK.com

Printed in Dunstable, United Kingdom